Quick Reference Guide

DDC ™

Microsoft Windows 3.1

IBM PC

D1165949

Karl Schwartz/Joanne Schwartz

Dictation Disc Company
14 East 38 Street, New York, NY 10016

ISBN: 1-56243-083-1

10   9   8   7   6   5   4   3

Printed in the United States of America

INTRODUCTION

The DDC Quick Reference Guide for Microsoft Windows 3.1 is designed to help you master any Windows operation without searching through a lengthy manual.

- Step-by-step instructions show how to easily perform Windows actions using a mouse.

- We explain basic mouse operations on the following page.

- We've included alternate keyboard methods and shortcuts to find faster ways for you to do your work. See Appendix B.

- To make the procedures easy to follow, the steps include the same graphic symbols that appear on your Windows screen.

- Topics are grouped so that related information is easy to find. See the Table of Contents in this section.

- We've provided a section that illustrates the basic concepts and terms you need to put Windows to work for you. See Appendix C.

Karl Schwartz
Joanne Schwartz

Editors:
Kristen Cassereau
Maria Reidelbach

Advisors:
Margaret Brown
David Phillips

Design and layout:
Karl Schwartz
Joanne Schwartz

BASIC MOUSE OPERATIONS

POINTING

- When you move the mouse, the ⏴ (pointer) moves and changes shape, depending upon its location.

CLICK ON

To click on an item,

1. Move the mouse pointer until it contacts the item.

2. Quickly press and release the left mouse button.

DOUBLE-CLICK ON

To double-click on an item,

1. Move the mouse pointer until it contacts the item.

2. Press left mouse button <u>twice</u> in rapid succession.

CLICK, HOLD AND DRAG

To click, hold and drag an item,

1. Move the mouse pointer until it contacts the item.

2. Press <u>and</u> hold the left mouse button while moving mouse. Release mouse button to complete the action.

NOTE: By default, the left mouse button is the primary button. You can change the primary mouse button and other mouse controls (see Customizing Mouse, page 134).

TABLE OF CONTENTS

Continued ...

iv

TABLE OF CONTENTS — Applications (continued)

Continued ...

V

TABLE OF CONTENTS — Program Manager (continued)

Continued ...

vi

TABLE OF CONTENTS — File Manager (continued)

Continued ...

TABLE OF CONTENTS (continued)

PRINT MANAGER

RECORDER

Continued ...

viii

TABLE OF CONTENTS — Recorder (continued)

Continued ...

TABLE OF CONTENTS — Object Linking and Embedding (OLE) (continued)

PIF EDITOR

APPENDIX A — Accessories

Continued ...

X

TABLE OF CONTENTS (continued)
APPENDIX B — Using the Keyboard

APPENDIX C — Concepts Glossary

INDEX

STARTING WINDOWS

FROM DOS PROMPT

DEFAULT

1. Type . . . . `W` `I` `N`

2. Press . . . . `⏎`

   Windows determines optimum operating mode based on the type of computer and the amount of memory.

STANDARD MODE

1. Type . . . . `W` `I` `N` `/` `S`

2. Press . . . . `⏎`

   for computers with 80286 or higher processors.

386 ENHANCED MODE

1. Type . . . . `W` `I` `N` `/` `3`

2. Press . . . . `⏎`

   for computers with 80386 or higher processors — provides optimum operating environment, including multitasking and use of virtual memory.

TO START WINDOWS AND IMMEDIATELY RUN AN APPLICATION:

1. Type . . . . `W` `I` `N`

2. Press . . . . `Space`

3. Type full program name.

   NOTE: If necessary, specify the exact location of the program file. For example, type C:\WP51\WP.EXE to load the WordPerfect program located on drive C: in directory WP51.

4. Press . . . . `⏎`

2

QUITTING WINDOWS
– Using Control-Menu

NOTE: *Before quitting Windows, you can specify whether or not to save the current desktop arrangement. See Using Program Manager's "Save Settings on Exit" Option, page 4.*
If Program Manager is not in view, see Selecting a Running Application, page 17.

IF Program Manager is a <u>window</u>,

1. Double-click on Program Manager's . . . . ⊟

2. Click on . . . . [OK]

OR

1. Click on Program Manager's . . . . ⊟
    to open its Control-menu.

2. Click on . . . . **Close**

3. Click on . . . . [OK]

IF Program Manager is an <u>icon</u> on the desktop,

1. Click on . . . . [icon]
    to open its Control-menu.

2. Click on . . . . **Close**

3. Click on . . . . [OK]

QUITTING WINDOWS
– Using File Menu

NOTE: Before quitting Windows, you can specify whether or not to save the current desktop arrangement. See Using Program Manager's "Save Settings on Exit" Option, page 4.

FROM PROGRAM MANAGER WINDOW

1. Click on . . . . **File**

2. Click on . . . . **Exit Windows**

3. Click on . . . . **OK**

DISPLAYING SYSTEM RESOURCES AND CURRENT OPERATING MODE

FROM PROGRAM MANAGER WINDOW

1. Click on . . . . **Help**

2. Click on . . . . **About Program Manager**
   Program Manager displays information about the current operating mode and available system resources.

3. Click on . . . . **OK**

USING PROGRAM MANAGER'S "SAVE SETTINGS ON EXIT" OPTION

NOTE: *When this option is selected (✓), Windows will save the arrangement of windows and icons, as they appear, when you quit Windows.*

FROM PROGRAM MANAGER WINDOW

1. Click on . . . . **Options**
2. Click on . . . . **Save Settings on Exit**
   to select (✓) or deselect.

Also see Saving Current Desktop Arrangement without Quitting Windows, below.

SAVING CURRENT DESKTOP ARRANGEMENT WITHOUT QUITTING WINDOWS

FROM PROGRAM MANAGER WINDOW

1. Click on . . . . **File**
2. Press and hold . . . . **Shift**
   and click on . . . . **Exit Windows**

MOVING A WINDOW OR ICON

TO MOVE A WINDOW:

1. Point to title bar of window to move.

2. Click, hold and drag mouse to move window to new location.

3. Release mouse button.

TO MOVE AN ICON:

1. Point to icon to move.

2. Click, hold and drag mouse to move icon to new location.

3. Release mouse button.

CHANGING THE SIZE OF A WINDOW

NOTE: A maximized window must be restored (page 7) before it can be sized.

1. Point to border or corner of window to size.
    Pointer becomes one of the following: ⇔ ⤢ ⇕.

2. Click, hold and drag mouse to resize window.

3. Release mouse button.

4. Repeat steps 1-3 until desired size is obtained.

6

MINIMIZING A WINDOW

NOTE: *When minimized, application windows are reduced to icons and placed on the bottom of the desktop (the area below all windows). Document windows, when minimized, are reduced to icons and placed within their application's borders.*

1. Click on the window's . . . . ▼

    NOTE: A maximized document window may not have a Minimize button. To minimize, use steps 1 and 2 below.

OR

1. Click on the window's . . . . ▭

    NOTE: The Control-menu button of a maximized document window is located on the left side of its application window's menu bar.

2. Click on . . . . **Minimize**

MAXIMIZING A WINDOW

NOTE: *Application windows will expand to full screen size. Document windows will expand to the limit of their application's window borders, but will not extend over their application's title and menu bar.*

TO MAXIMIZE WINDOW USING MAXIMIZE BUTTON:

• Click on the window's . . . . ▲

> *NOTE: After a window is maximized, the Maximize button is replaced with a ⬍ (Restore button).*

TO MAXIMIZE WINDOW USING CONTROL-MENU:

1. Click on the window's . . . . ▬

2. Click on . . . . **Maximize**

> *NOTE: After a window is maximized, the Maximize button is replaced with a ⬍ (Restore button).*

TO MAXIMIZE WINDOW USING TITLE BAR:

• Double-click on the window's. . . . .   Title bar

> *NOTE: After a window is maximized, the Maximize button is replaced with a ⬍ (Restore button).*

RESTORING A MAXIMIZED WINDOW

NOTE: *The Restore button of a maximized application window is located at the top right corner of its window. The Restore button of a maximized document window is located on the right side of its application's menu bar.*

FROM A MAXIMIZED WINDOW

• Click on maximized window's . . . .

> *NOTE: After a window is restored, the Restore button is replaced with a ▲ (Maximize button).*

8

SELECTING OPTIONS IN A DIALOG BOX

Also see Parts of a Dialog Box, page 216.

TO SELECT A LIST BOX:

- Click anywhere in list box.

  Selected list box contains an outlined item.

TO OPEN A DROP-DOWN LIST:

- Click on . . . . list name's ⊡

TO SELECT ONE ITEM IN A LIST BOX:

- Click on item.

  Selected item is highlighted.

  IF item is not in view,

  - Click on scroll arrows, then execute step 1.

TO SELECT CONSECUTIVE ITEMS IN A LIST BOX:

1. Click on first item.

2. Press . . . . **Shift**
   <u>and</u> click on last item in group to select.

TO SELECT MULTIPLE ITEMS IN A LIST BOX:

- Press . . . . **Ctrl**
  <u>and</u> click on each item.

TO TYPE DATA IN AN EMPTY TEXT BOX:

1. Click anywhere in . . . . . text box name's [   ]

2. Type the data.

Continued ...

SELECTING OPTIONS IN A DIALOG BOX (continued)

TO EDIT DATA IN A TEXT BOX:

1. Click on desired character
   position in . . . . text box name's | data |

   IF necessary, use edit keys to remove existing
      characters to the right (Del) or left (Backspace) of
      insertion point.

2. Type new data.

TO REPLACE DATA IN A TEXT BOX:

1. Double-click on data
   to replace in . . . . text box name's |▓data▓|

   Existing data is highlighted.

2. Type new data.

TO SELECT/DESELECT A CHECK BOX:

• Click on . . . . ☐ option name
   to select (☒).

   OR

   Click on . . . . ☒ option name
   to deselect (☐).

   NOTE: More than one check box may be selected in a group.

TO SELECT AN OPTION BUTTON:

• Click on . . . . ○ option name
   to select (◉).

   NOTE: Only one option button may be selected in a group.

TO SELECT A COMMAND BUTTON:

• Click on . . . . [**Command name**]

   Selected command button carries out the command action.

10

LOCATING FILES

NOTE: *The dialog box options below appear after you choose a command (such as Browse or Open). The options may vary depending on the command used.*

FROM DIALOG BOX

TO LIST FILES STORED ON A DIFFERENT DRIVE:

    a) Click on . . . . Dri̱ves: ⬇️

    b) Click on desired drive.

TO LIST FILES STORED IN A DIFFERENT DIRECTORY:

    • Double-click on a directory name in D̲irectories list box.

TO LIST FILES OF A DIFFERENT TYPE:

    a) Click on . . . . List File of T̲ype: ⬇️

    b) Click on file type to list.

    OR

    a) Double-click in . . . . File N̲ame: ⬜

    b) Type a new filespec.

        EXAMPLE: **.INI — to list only files that have an INI filename extension.*

• Double-click on a filename in File N̲ame list box.

OR

1. Double-click in . . . . File N̲ame: ⬜

2. Type a filename.

    EXAMPLE: *C:\YOURDIR\YOURFILE.TXT — example using a full pathname.*

3. Click on . . . . [OK]

SCROLLING
— Moving an Area of Data into View

ONE CHARACTER LEFT OR RIGHT:
- Click on left or right scroll arrow.

ONE LINE UP OR DOWN:
- Click on up or down scroll arrow.

TO THE BEGINNING OF A LINE OR LIST:
- Click, hold and drag horizontal scroll box to the extreme left of scroll bar.

TO THE END OF A LINE OR LIST:
- Click, hold and drag horizontal scroll box to the extreme right of scroll bar.

TO THE BEGINNING OF A DOCUMENT OR LIST:
- Click, hold and drag vertical scroll box to the top of scroll bar.

TO THE END OF A DOCUMENT OR LIST:
- Click, hold and drag vertical scroll box to the bottom of scroll bar.

ONE SCREEN UP:
- Click on vertical scroll bar above scroll box.

ONE SCREEN DOWN:
- Click on vertical scroll bar below scroll box.

ONE SCREEN RIGHT:
- Click on horizontal scroll bar right of scroll box.

ONE SCREEN LEFT:
- Click on horizontal scroll bar left of scroll box.

RUNNING AN APPLICATION FROM A GROUP WINDOW

FROM PROGRAM MANAGER WINDOW

IF   group containing application is an <u>icon</u>,

  • Double-click on desired . . . .
    then execute step 1.   group name

IF   group containing application is <u>hidden</u>,

  a) Click on . . . .   **Window**

  b) Click on desired group name, then execute
     step 1.

FROM GROUP WINDOW CONTAINING APPLICATION TO RUN:

1.   Double-click on desired program item icon.

RUNNING APPLICATIONS AUTOMATICALLY ON STARTUP

*NOTE: The applications in the Startup group will run in the order in
         which they appear in the group. By default, the predefined
         Startup group is empty.*

FROM PROGRAM MANAGER WINDOW

1.   Arrange groups so that the group window containing
     the application and the Startup group is in view.

2.   Click, hold and drag desired program item icon from
     its group onto the Startup group.

3.   Release mouse button.

*NOTE: To run application as an icon on startup, see Changing
         Properties of a Program Item, page 49.*

RUNNING A NON-WINDOWS APPLICATION FROM MS-DOS PROMPT

FROM PROGRAM MANAGER MAIN GROUP WINDOW

1. Double-click on . . . . 🖳

MS-DOS
Prompt

FROM DOS PROMPT

2. Type MS-DOS command or program name.

   NOTE: <u>*CAUTION*</u>: *Do not run programs (such as disk and file utilities) or commands (such as CHKDSK /F) that might change the file allocation table. Windows <u>must</u> be exited before you run such programs or commands.*

3. Press . . . . ↵

TO RETURN TO WINDOWS AND LEAVE MS-DOS RUNNING:

FROM DOS PROMPT

• Press . . . . **Alt** + **Tab**

TO RETURN TO WINDOWS AND QUIT MS-DOS:

FROM DOS PROMPT

1. Type . . . . **E** **X** **I** **T**

2. Press . . . . ↵

RUNNING AN APPLICATION USING THE RUN COMMAND

FROM PROGRAM MANAGER OR FILE MANAGER WINDOW

1. Click on . . . . **File**

2. Click on . . . . **Run...**

3. Type a full pathname, program filename, and an optional document name.

   EXAMPLE: C:\WP51\WP.EXE JONES.LTR — to run WordPerfect and load specific document file.

   OR

   a) Click on . . . . `Browse...`

   b) Double-click on filename to run in File <u>N</u>ame list box.
   See Locating Files, page 10.

TO RUN APPLICATION AS AN ICON:

- Click on . . . . ☐ Run <u>M</u>inimized to select (☒).

4. Click on . . . . `OK`

RUNNING AN APPLICATION USING FILE ICONS

FROM FILE MANAGER WINDOW

1. Select drive and directory containing file to run.

    See Selecting a Disk Drive, page 52.
    See Changing the Current Directory, page 53.

TO RUN THE APPLICATION:

FROM DIRECTORY CONTENTS LIST

(The right side of directory window)

2. Double-click on an application file's . . . . . .

    NOTE: Application files have .EXE, .COM, .PIF, or .BAT filename extensions.

OR

TO RUN THE APPLICATION AND OPEN A DATA FILE:

FROM DIRECTORY CONTENTS LIST

(The right side of directory window)

2. Double-click on an associated file's . . . .

    See Associating Data Files with Applications, page 81.

    OR

    a) Click, hold and drag a data file's . . . .

        onto an application file's . . . .

        NOTE: The data file must have been created by the application file.

    b) Release mouse button.

16

RUNNING A NON-WINDOWS APPLICATION IN A WINDOW

NOTE: *Requires 386 enhanced mode.*

FROM A FULL-SCREEN, NON-WINDOWS APPLICATION

TO SWITCH TO WINDOW MODE:

- Press . . . . `Alt` + `↵`

TO SWITCH BACK TO FULL-SCREEN MODE:

- Press . . . . `Alt` + `↵`

NOTE: *It may be necessary to press Esc (to cancel a Scroll or Mark command) before returning to full-screen mode.*

SELECTING A RUNNING APPLICATION

TO SELECT AN APPLICATION RUNNING IN A WINDOW:

• Click anywhere on the application window.

TO OPEN AN APPLICATION RUNNING AS AN ICON:

• Double-click on the application icon.

TO SELECT OR OPEN AN APPLICATION RUNNING IN A HIDDEN WINDOW OR ICON:

1. Double-click on the desktop.

   NOTE: The desktop is the area below all windows.

   OR

   a) Click on any application window's . . . . ⊟

   b) Click on . . . . **Switch To...**

2. Double-click on desired application name in Task List.

TO MOVE SELECTION QUICKLY AMONG RUNNING APPLICATIONS:

1. Press and hold . . . . **Alt**

   while pressing and releasing . . . . **Tab**
   until name of desired application is displayed
   or its title is highlighted.

2. Release keys.

18

ARRANGING APPLICATION WINDOWS AND ICONS

1. Double-click on the desktop.

   NOTE: The desktop is the area below all windows.

   OR

   a) Click on any application window's . . . . ⊟

   b) Click on . . . . **Sw̲itch To...**

2. Click on one of the following:

   ● . . . . | **C̲ascade** |

   (Arranges application windows in an overlapping order and places application icons on the bottom of the desktop.)

   ● . . . . | **T̲ile** |

   (Arranges application windows in a side-by-side order and places application icons on the bottom of the desktop.)

   ● . . . . | **A̲rrange Icons** |

   (Places application icons on the bottom of the desktop without changing the arrangement of application windows.)

SELECTING A DOCUMENT WINDOW

NOTE: Document windows are found within the borders of their application window.

FROM ANY APPLICATION CONTAINING
DOCUMENT WINDOWS

- Click anywhere on the document window.

TO SELECT A <u>HIDDEN</u> DOCUMENT WINDOW:

1. Click on . . . . **Window**

2. Click on name of document to select.

**TO MOVE SELECTION QUICKLY AMONG
DOCUMENT WINDOWS:**

- Press . . . . **Ctrl** + **Tab**
  until title of desired document window is highlighted.

CLOSING A DOCUMENT WINDOW

NOTE: In most cases, closing a document window removes the document from its application window.

FROM ANY APPLICATION CONTAINING
DOCUMENT WINDOWS

- Double-click on the document window's . . . . . 🗕

OR

1. Click on the document window's . . . . 🗕

2. Click on . . . . **Close**

20

OPENING A DOCUMENT ICON

*NOTE: Document icons are found within the borders of their
application window. When opened, document icons
become document windows.*

FROM ANY APPLICATION CONTAINING DOCUMENT ICONS

• Double-click on document icon.

OR

1. Click on document icon to open its Control-menu.

2. Click on . . . . **Restore**
    to open to its previous size.

    OR

    Click on . . . . **Maximize**
    to open to its largest size.

TO OPEN A <u>HIDDEN</u> DOCUMENT ICON:

1. Click on . . . . **Window**

2. Click on name of document to open.

CLOSING A DOCUMENT ICON

NOTE: *In most cases, closing a document icon removes the*
document from its application window.

FROM ANY APPLICATION CONTAINING DOCUMENT ICONS

1. Click on document icon to open its Control-menu.

2. Click on . . . . **Close**

TO CLOSE A <u>HIDDEN</u> DOCUMENT ICON:

1. Click on . . . . **Window**

2. Click on . . . . **Tile**

3. Click on document icon to open its Control-menu.

4. Click on . . . . **Close**

22

ARRANGING DOCUMENT WINDOWS AND ICONS

FROM ANY APPLICATION CONTAINING DOCUMENT WINDOWS OR ICONS

1. Click on . . . . **Window**

2. Click on one of the following:

- . . . . **Cascade**

  (Arranges document windows in an overlapping order and places document icons at the bottom of their application window.)

- . . . . **Tile**

  (Arranges document windows in a side-by-side order and places document icons at the bottom of their application window.)

- . . . . **Arrange Icons**

  (Arranges document icons at the bottom of their application window without changing the arrangement of document windows.)

  NOTE: This option may not be available for all applications.

CLOSING AN APPLICATION WINDOW OR ICON

*NOTE: When closed, an application window or icon is removed
        from the desktop. Closing the Program Manager application
        window or icon will end the Windows session.*

TO CLOSE AN APPLICATION WINDOW USING FILE MENU:

1. Click on . . . . **File**

2. Click on . . . . **Exit**

**TO CLOSE AN APPLICATION WINDOW USING
CONTROL-MENU:**

• Double-click on application window's . . . . ⊟

OR

1. Click on application window's . . . . ⊟

2. Click on . . . . **Close**

TO CLOSE AN APPLICATION ICON:

1. Click on icon to open its Control-menu.

2. Click on . . . . **Close**

TO CLOSE A <u>HIDDEN</u> APPLICATION WINDOW OR ICON:

1. Double-click on the desktop.

   NOTE: The desktop is the area below all windows.

   OR

   a) Click on any application window's . . . . ⊟

   b) Click on . . . . **Switch To...**

2. Click on name of application to close in Task List.

3. Click on . . . . `End Task`

OPENING DATA FILES – Retrieving Files

FROM A WINDOWS APPLICATION

1. Click on . . . . **File**

2. Click on . . . . **Open...**

TO LIST FILES STORED ON A DIFFERENT DRIVE:

    a) Click on . . . . Dri̲ves: ⬇

    b) Click on desired drive.

TO LIST FILES STORED IN A DIFFERENT DIRECTORY:

    • Double-click on a directory name in D̲irectories list box.

TO LIST FILES OF A DIFFERENT TYPE:

    a) Click on . . . . List File of T̲ype: ⬇

    b) Click on file type to list.

    OR

    a) Double-click in . . . . File N̲ame: ▭

    b) Type a new filespec.

        EXAMPLE: *.INI — to list only files that have an INI filename extension.

3. Double-click on filename to open in File N̲ame list box.

    OR

    a) Double-click in . . . . File N̲ame: ▭

    b) Type name of file to open.

        EXAMPLES: CHAPT1.TXT — example using a filename.
                    C:\MYBOOKS\CHAPT1.TXT — example using a full pathname.

    c) Click on . . . . **OK**

SAVING AND NAMING DATA FILES
– For New Files or Renaming an Existing File

FROM A WINDOWS APPLICATION

1. Click on . . . . **File**
2. Click on . . . . **Save As...**

TO SAVE FILE TO A DIFFERENT DRIVE:

   a) Click on . . . . Dri_ves: ⬇
   b) Click on desired drive.

TO SAVE FILE IN A DIFFERENT DIRECTORY:

   • Double-click on a directory name in _Directories
     list box.

3. Double-click in . . . . File _Name: [＿＿＿＿＿]
4. Type a filename.

   EXAMPLES: _CHAPT1.TXT_ — _example using a filename._
   C:\MYBOOK\CHAPT1.TXT — _example using a full
   pathname._

5. Click on . . . . [**OK**]

SAVING AN EXISTING DATA FILE

NOTE: _Saves file under the same name, to the drive and directory
   to which it was last saved. If the file has not been named,
   see Saving and Naming Data Files, above._

FROM A WINDOWS APPLICATION

1. Click on . . . . **File**
2. Click on . . . . **Save**

PRINTING AN OPEN DATA FILE

FROM A WINDOWS APPLICATION

1. Click on . . . . **File**

2. Click on . . . . **Print**

3. Select desired options from dialog box.
   See Selecting Options in a Dialog Box, page 8.

4. Click on . . . . `OK`

SELECTING TEXT

FROM A WINDOWS APPLICATION WORKSPACE

1. Point to first character of text to select.

2. Click, hold and drag mouse to extend
   selection highlight.

3. Release mouse button when desired text
   is highlighted.

TO CANCEL SELECTION BLOCK:

   • Click anywhere in document workspace.

4. Execute desired command.

   *NOTE: Commands that can be applied to selected text include
   cut, copy and delete.
   See Cutting (Deleting) Data and Placing It in the
   Clipboard — For Windows Applications, page 27.
   See Copying Data and Placing It in the Clipboard —
   For Windows Applications, page 28.*

CUTTING (DELETING) DATA AND PLACING IT IN THE CLIPBOARD
— For Windows Applications

NOTE: Data placed in the Clipboard replaces existing Clipboard data.

FROM A WINDOWS APPLICATION

1. Select data to cut.
2. Click on . . . . **Edit**
3. Click on . . . . **Cut**

UNDOING A COMMAND

NOTE: To successfully undo a command, undo before another command is entered. Not all commands can be undone.

1. Click on . . . . **Edit**
2. Click on . . . . **Undo**

COPYING DATA AND PLACING IT IN THE CLIPBOARD
– For Windows Applications

NOTE: Data placed in the Clipboard replaces existing Clipboard data.

FROM A WINDOWS APPLICATION

1.   Select data to copy.

2.   Click on . . . . **Edit**

3.   Click on . . . . **Copy**

COPYING DATA AND PLACING IT IN THE CLIPBOARD – For Non-Windows Applications Running in a Window

*NOTE: Requires 386 enhanced mode.
Data placed in the Clipboard replaces existing Clipboard data.*

FROM A WINDOWED, NON-WINDOWS APPLICATION

1.   Click on application window's . . . . ⊟

2.   Click on . . . . **Edit** ▶

3.   Click on . . . . **Mark**

4.   Select data to copy.

5.   Click on application window's . . . . ⊟

6.   Click on . . . . **Edit** ▶

7.   Click on . . . . **Copy**

COPYING ENTIRE SCREEN TO CLIPBOARD
— For Windows or Non-Windows Applications

NOTE: *Data placed in the Clipboard replaces existing Clipboard data.*
These steps can be used in any mode except for a non-Windows application running in <u>graphics mode.</u>

FROM A WINDOWS OR NON-WINDOWS APPLICATION

1. Place data to be copied within view on screen.

2. Press . . . . **Prnt Scrn**

   NOTE: For some keyboards, it may be necessary to press Shift + Print Screen or Alt + Print Screen.

COPYING ONLY THE ACTIVE WINDOW TO CLIPBOARD

NOTE: *Requires 386 enhanced mode.*
Non-Windows applications <u>must</u> be running in a window (page 16).
Data placed in the Clipboard replaces existing Clipboard data.

FROM ANY APPLICATION RUNNING IN A WINDOW

1. Place data to be copied within active window.

2. Press . . . . **Alt** + **Prnt Scrn**

   NOTE: For some keyboards, it may be necessary to press Shift + Print Screen.

PASTING DATA FROM CLIPBOARD
– Into a Windows Application

*NOTE: Data must be appropriate for the receiving application.
Make sure that data has been placed in the Clipboard.*

FROM A WINDOWS APPLICATION

1. Run or select application that will receive data.

2. Click on location where data is to be pasted.

3. Click on . . . . **Edit**

4. Click on . . . . **Paste**

PASTING DATA FROM CLIPBOARD
– Into a Non-Windows Application Running in a Window

*NOTE: Requires 386 enhanced mode.
Data must be appropriate for the receiving application.
Make sure that data has been placed in the Clipboard.*

FROM A WINDOWED, NON-WINDOWS APPLICATION

1. Place insertion point where data is to be pasted.

2. Click on application window's . . . . ▭

3. Click on . . . . **Edit** ▸

4. Click on . . . . **Paste**

PASTING TEXT FROM CLIPBOARD

— Into a Non-Windows Application Running Full-Screen

NOTE: *Data must be appropriate for the receiving application. Make sure that <u>text</u> has been placed in the Clipboard.*

1. Run or select non-Windows application that will receive text.

2. Place insertion point where <u>text</u> is to be pasted.

3. Press . . . . |Alt| + |Esc| to switch to Windows.

   NOTE: It is necessary to switch to Windows and access the target application's Control-menu, since non-Windows full-screen programs do not have a Paste command.

4. Press . . . . |Alt| + |Esc| until title of target application icon is highlighted.

5. Click on target application icon to open its Control-menu.

IF in 386 enhanced mode,

   • Click on . . . . **<u>E</u>dit** ▸

6. Click on . . . . **<u>P</u>aste**

NOTE: *To return to the application that received the text, double-click on its icon.*

32

USING THE CLIPBOARD VIEWER

FROM PROGRAM MANAGER MAIN GROUP WINDOW

*   Double-click on . . . .

    Clipboard
    Viewer

TO DELETE THE CONTENTS OF CLIPBOARD:

a) Click on . . . . **Edit**

b) Click on . . . . **Delete**

c) Click on . . . . ‎ OK

TO VIEW CLIPBOARD DATA FORMATS:

a) Click on . . . . **Display**

b) Click on one of the following:

*   . . . . **Auto**

*   . . . . **Text**

*   . . . . **OEM Text**

*   . . . . **Bitmap**

> *NOTE: Clipboard uses various formats for transferring
> information. The options in the Display menu will
> depend on the application that transferred the data
> to Clipboard.*

TO SAVE THE CONTENTS OF CLIPBOARD:
See Saving and Naming Data Files, page 25.

TO RETRIEVE A CLIPBOARD FILE:
See Opening Data Files — Retrieving Files, page 24.

RECEIVING MESSAGES FROM UNSELECTED RUNNING APPLICATIONS

NOTE: When an application sends a message, its title flashes and a beeping sound may be heard.

• Select flashing application window (page 17).

OR

• Open flashing application icon (page 17).

CLOSING A WINDOWS APPLICATION

See Closing an Application Window or Icon, page 23.

CLOSING NON-WINDOWS APPLICATIONS

NOTE: All non-Windows applications must be closed in order to quit Windows.

• Refer to application's documentation.

NOTE: If a non-Windows application will not close, it may be possible — as a last resort — to terminate the application from Windows. (See Changing Settings of a Running Non-Windows Application, page 34.)

CHANGING SETTINGS OF A RUNNING NON-WINDOWS APPLICATION

NOTE: Requires 386 enhanced mode.

IF   application is running in a <u>window</u>,

1. Click on application window's . . . . ⊟

2. Click on . . . . **Se_ttings...**

IF   application is running as an <u>icon</u>,

1. Click on icon.

2. Click on . . . . **Se_ttings...**

TO SWITCH BETWEEN RUNNING APPLICATION IN A WINDOW OR FULL SCREEN:

- Click on . . . . ◯ <u>W</u>indow

   OR

   Click on . . . . ◯ F<u>u</u>ll Screen
   to select (◉).

TO CONTROL SHARING OF SYSTEM RESOURCES:

- Click on . . . . ☐ E<u>x</u>clusive

   AND/OR

   Click on . . . . ☐ <u>B</u>ackground
   to select (☒).

Continued ...

CHANGING SETTINGS OF A RUNNING
NON-WINDOWS APPLICATION (continued)

TO CONTROL HOW FAST APPLICATION WILL RUN:

a) Click in . . . . Foreground: [ ]

b) Type a number (1-1000).

> NOTE: Number represents a time slice measured
> in milliseconds.

c) Click in . . . . Background: [ ]

d) Type a number (1-1000).

> NOTE: Number represents a time slice measured
> in milliseconds.

TO TERMINATE THE APPLICATION:

NOTE: CAUTION: Only use this option when it is not possible to
exit the program in a normal way. After using this option,
you should quit Windows and restart your system before
using any application in Windows.

a) Click on . . . . [Terminate...]

b) Click on . . . . [OK]

OR

Click on . . . . [Cancel]

3. Click on . . . . [OK]

SELECT/OPEN PROGRAM MANAGER

*NOTE: Central to the operations performed in Windows, Program
Manager is used to organize and run applications. When
Windows is started, it automatically runs Program Manager,
which runs as long as Windows is in use.*

TO SELECT PROGRAM MANAGER WINDOW:

• Click anywhere on Program Manager window.

TO OPEN PROGRAM MANAGER ICON:

• Double-click on . . . .

Program
Manager

**TO SELECT OR OPEN PROGRAM MANAGER RUNNING
IN A <u>HIDDEN</u> WINDOW OR ICON:**

1. Double-click on the desktop.

   NOTE: The desktop is the area below all windows.

   OR

   a) Click on any application window's . . . .

   b) Click on . . . . **S<u>w</u>itch To...**

2. Double-click on Program Manager's name in
   Task List.

TO QUICKLY SELECT OR OPEN PROGRAM MANAGER:

1. Press and hold . . . . **Alt**

   <u>while</u> pressing and releasing . . . . **Tab**
   until Program Manager's name is displayed or
   its title is highlighted.

2. Release keys.

MINIMIZING OR RETAINING PROGRAM MANAGER'S WINDOW WHEN RUNNING AN APPLICATION

NOTE: *When this option is selected (✓), Program Manager will run as an icon whenever an application is started. The Program Manager icon will be placed on the bottom of the desktop (the area below all windows).*

FROM PROGRAM MANAGER WINDOW

1. Click on . . . . **Options**

2. Click on . . . . **Minimize on Use**
    to select (✓) or deselect.

ARRANGING GROUP WINDOWS

See Arranging Document Windows and Icons, page 22.
See Moving a Window or Icon, page 5.
See Changing the Size of a Window, page 5.

SELECTING A GROUP WINDOW

NOTE: *Group windows are found within the borders of the*
         Program Manager window.

FROM PROGRAM MANAGER WINDOW

• Click anywhere on the group window.

TO SELECT A <u>HIDDEN</u> GROUP WINDOW:

1. Click on . . . . **Window**

2. Click on name of group to select.

TO MOVE SELECTION QUICKLY AMONG GROUP WINDOWS:

• Press . . . . **Ctrl** + **Tab**
  until title of desired group window is highlighted.

Also see Opening a Group Icon, page 39.

MINIMIZING A GROUP WINDOW

NOTE: *When minimized, a group window becomes a group icon*
         that is placed within the Program Manager window.
         Minimizing group windows conserves system memory.

FROM PROGRAM MANAGER WINDOW

• Click on the group window's . . . . ▼

OR

• Double-click on the group window's . . . . □

OR

1. Click on the group window's . . . . □

2. Click on . . . . **Close**

OPENING A GROUP ICON

NOTE: *Group icons are found within the borders of the Program Manager window. When opened, group icons become group windows.*

FROM PROGRAM MANAGER WINDOW

• Double-click on desired . . . .

group name

OR

1. Click on desired . . . . to open its Control-menu.

group name

2. Click on . . . . **Restore** to open to its previous size.

   OR

   Click on . . . . **Maximize** to open to its largest size.

TO OPEN A HIDDEN GROUP ICON:

1. Click on . . . . **Window**
2. Click on the name of group to open.

40

CREATING A NEW GROUP

FROM PROGRAM MANAGER WINDOW

1. Click on .... **File**

2. Click on .... **New...**

3. Click on .... ○ Program Group
   to select (◉).

4. Click on .... | OK |

5. Type group description in . . . Ｕnderline Description: [   ]

   NOTE: The group description will appear as the
   title of the new group window.

6. Click on .... | OK |

DELETING A GROUP

NOTE: *Program item icons must be removed before a <u>group</u>*
<u>window</u> can be deleted. <u>Group</u> <u>icons</u>, however, can be
deleted at any time. In this case, all program item icons
are deleted with the group. Application files will not be
removed from the disk drive. For information about these
elements, see Windows — An Overview, page 212.

FROM PROGRAM MANAGER WINDOW

IF group to delete is a <u>window</u>,

1. • Click on group window to delete.

   • Move or delete all program item icons, then
     execute step 2.

     See Deleting a Program Item Icon from a Group, page 46.
     See Moving a Program Item Icon to Another Group,
     page 45.

OR

1. Click on . . . .
    to delete.

group name

    NOTE: Ignore display of group icon's Control-menu.

2. Click on . . . . **File**

3. Click on . . . . **Delete**

4. Click on . . . . Yes

CHANGING THE TITLE OF A GROUP

FROM PROGRAM MANAGER WINDOW

IF   group to rename is a <u>window</u>,

- Click on group window's . . . . ▼

    NOTE: A group window must be minimized (reduced to an icon) before its title can be changed.

1. Click on . . . . ⊞⊞⊞
   to change.   group name

   NOTE: Ignore display of group icon's Control-menu.

2. Click on . . . . **File**

3. Click on . . . . **Properties...**

4. Type a new title in . . . . <u>D</u>escription: ▢

5. Click on . . . . [OK]

ARRANGING GROUP ICONS

Arranges group icons near bottom of Program Manager window.

FROM PROGRAM MANAGER WINDOW

1. Click on any group icon.

    NOTE: Ignore display of group icon's Control-menu.

2. Click on . . . . **Window**

3. Click on . . . . **Arrange Icons**

ARRANGING PROGRAM ITEM ICONS

FROM PROGRAM MANAGER WINDOW

1. Click on group window containing program item icons to arrange.

2. Click on . . . . **Window**

3. Click on . . . . **Arrange Icons**

Also see Setting the Automatic Arrangement of Program Item Icons, page 44.

SETTING THE AUTOMATIC ARRANGEMENT OF PROGRAM ITEM ICONS

NOTE: *When this option is selected (✓), Windows automatically arranges all program item icons whenever a group window is sized or a program item icon is added or moved.*

FROM PROGRAM MANAGER WINDOW

1. Click on . . . . **Options**

2. Click on . . . . **A̲uto Arrange**
   to select (✓) or deselect.

COPYING A PROGRAM ITEM ICON TO ANOTHER GROUP

FROM PROGRAM MANAGER WINDOW

1. Arrange source and destination groups so that both are in view.

IF source group is an <u>icon</u>,

   • Double-click on source . . . . ⊞
     to open.   group name

2. Press and hold . . . . |**Ctrl**|
   <u>and</u> click, hold and drag program item icon onto destination group.

3. Release mouse button and key.

MOVING A PROGRAM ITEM ICON WITHIN A GROUP WINDOW

FROM A PROGRAM MANAGER GROUP WINDOW

1. Point to program item icon to move.

2. Click, hold and drag icon to new location.

3. Release mouse button.

NOTE: If the Auto Arrange option is selected, the moved icon is inserted and existing icons are shifted. See Setting the Automatic Arrangement of Program Items Icons, page 44.

MOVING A PROGRAM ITEM ICON TO ANOTHER GROUP

FROM PROGRAM MANAGER WINDOW

1. Arrange source and destination groups so that both are in view.

IF source group is an <u>icon</u>,

• Double-click on source . . . .
  to open.

group name

2. Click, hold and drag program item icon onto destination group.

3. Release mouse button.

CHANGING THE TITLE OF A PROGRAM ITEM ICON

FROM PROGRAM MANAGER WINDOW

1. Select group window (page 38) or open group icon (page 39) containing program item to change.

2. Click on desired program item icon.

3. Click on . . . . **File**

4. Click on . . . . **Properties...**

5. Type a new title in . . . . Description: [   ]

6. Click on . . . . [OK]

DELETING A PROGRAM ITEM ICON FROM A GROUP

NOTE: This procedure will not remove the application from the disk drive.

FROM PROGRAM MANAGER WINDOW

1. Select group window (page 38) or open group icon (page 39) containing program item icon to delete.

2. Click on desired program item icon.

3. Click on . . . . **File**

4. Click on . . . . **Delete**

5. Click on . . . . [**Yes**]

ADDING A NEW PROGRAM ITEM TO A GROUP

FROM PROGRAM MANAGER WINDOW

1. Select group window (page 38) or open group icon (page 39) that will receive new program item icon.

2. Click on . . . . **File**

3. Click on . . . . **New...**

4. Click on . . . . [OK]

5. Type program item
   description in . . . . <u>D</u>escription: [   ]

   NOTE: Description will become title below program item icon.

6. Click in . . . . <u>C</u>ommand Line: [   ]

   • Type a filename.

   NOTE: Type a complete application filename, an optional data filename, or the name of an associated data file. EXAMPLES:
   PROGNAME.EXE — when located in the current directory.
   C:\WP5\WP.EXE — when located in another directory.
   C:\WP5\WP.EXE MYDATA.FIL — to load a specified document.
   C:\TODO.TXT — when data file is associated with an application.

   OR

   a) Click on . . . . [Browse...]

   b) Double-click on program or associated data filename in File <u>N</u>ame list box.

   See Locating Files, page 10.

Continued ...

ADDING A NEW PROGRAM ITEM TO A GROUP
(continued)

TO SPECIFY THE WORKING DIRECTORY WHEN THE APPLICATION IS RUNNING:

   a) Click in .... <u>W</u>orking Directory: [   ]

   b) Type a directory path.

     EXAMPLE: C:\WPDOC

     NOTE: If no directory is specified, Windows adds the directory of the program file when the dialog box is closed.

TO SPECIFY A SHORTCUT KEY TO USE WHEN THE APPLICATION IS RUNNING:

     NOTE: The shortcut key can be used to switch quickly to the application if it is running.

   a) Click in .... <u>S</u>hortcut Key: [   ]

   b) Press a key (character or number).

     NOTE: By default, Windows adds Ctrl + Alt before the key you pressed. To choose another combination, press the entire key combination (i.e., Ctrl + Shift + A).

TO RUN APPLICATION AS AN ICON ON STARTUP:

   • Click on .... ☐ <u>R</u>un Minimized
   to select (☒).

7. Click on .... [OK]

   New program item icon appears in group.

CHANGING PROPERTIES OF A PROGRAM ITEM

FROM A PROGRAM MANAGER GROUP WINDOW

1. Click on program item icon to change.

2. Click on . . . . **File**

3. Click on . . . . **Properties...**

TO CHANGE THE DESCRIPTION:

- Type a new program item
  description in . . . . **Description:** [   ]

TO CHANGE COMMAND LINE:

a) Click in . . . . **Command Line:** [   ]

b) Type a filename.

> *NOTE: Type a complete application filename, an optional
> data filename, or the name of an associated data
> file. EXAMPLES:*
> *PROGNAME.EXE — when located in the current
> directory.*
> *C:\WP5\WP.EXE — when located in another directory.*
> *C:\WP5\WP.EXE MYDATA.FIL — to load a
> specified document.*
> *C:\TODO.TXT — when data file is associated with an
> application.*

OR

a) Click on . . . . [**Browse...**]

b) Double-click on program or associated data
   filename in File Name list box.
   See Locating Files, page 10.

Continued ...

50

CHANGING PROPERTIES OF A PROGRAM ITEM
(continued)

TO CHANGE OR SPECIFY THE WORKING DIRECTORY WHEN THE APPLICATION IS RUNNING:

a) Click in . . . . <u>W</u>orking Directory: [_____]

b) Type a new, or delete existing, directory path.

NOTE: If the directory is removed, the Windows directory will become the current directory when the application is run.

TO CHANGE OR SPECIFY A SHORTCUT KEY TO USE WHEN THE APPLICATION IS RUNNING:

NOTE: The shortcut key can be used to switch quickly to the application if it is running.

a) Click in . . . . <u>S</u>hortcut Key: [_____]

b) Press a key (character or number).

NOTE: By default, Windows adds Ctrl + Alt before the key you pressed. To choose another combination, press the entire key combination (i.e., Ctrl + Shift + A).

TO RUN APPLICATION AS AN ICON ON STARTUP:

• Click on . . . . ☐ <u>R</u>un Minimized to select (☒).

4. Click on . . . . [OK]

to accept changes and return to Program Manager.

CHANGING A PROGRAM ITEM ICON

FROM A PROGRAM MANAGER GROUP WINDOW

1. Click on program item icon to change.

2. Click on . . . . **File**

3. Click on . . . . **Properties...**

4. Click on . . . . `Change Icon...`

TO CHANGE THE ICON LIST:

- Type path and name
  of source file in . . . . File **N**ame: [   ]

  EXAMPLE: C:\WINDOWS\MORICONS.DLL

  OR

  a) Click on . . . . `Browse...`

  b) Double-click on filename containing icons in
     File **N**ame list box.

     See Locating Files, page 10.

  *NOTE: Icons may be found in files with .EXE, .ICO, or .DLL
  filename extensions. MORICONS.DLL contains
  non-Windows application icons, and PROGMAN.EXE
  contains Windows application icons.*

5. Double-click on desired icon.

6. Click on . . . . `OK`

   to return to Program Manager Window.

STARTING FILE MANAGER

FROM PROGRAM MANAGER MAIN GROUP WINDOW

- Double-click on . . . .

File Manager

NOTE: *The first time File Manager is started it displays a*
directory window that shows the available disk
drives, the directory structure and the contents of
the current directory. For information about the
parts of the directory window, see File Manager —
An Overview, page 218.

SELECTING A DISK DRIVE

NOTE: *The current drive icon, in the drive list area, is surrounded*
by a rectangle.

FROM FILE MANAGER WINDOW

- Click on a drive icon in the drive list area.

NOTE: *File Manager searches the selected drive and displays*
contents of that drive as determined by the selected view
(page 59). To stop the search, press Esc.

CHANGING THE CURRENT DIRECTORY

NOTE: *The current directory, in the directory tree, appears as an* 📂 *(open folder).*
             To view all directories and subdirectories, see Expanding Directory Levels, page 54.

FROM FILE MANAGER WINDOW

FROM DIRECTORY TREE
(The left half of the directory window)

* Click on a directory name's . . . . 📁
  to make current.

  File Manager updates directory contents list.

OR

FROM DIRECTORY CONTENTS LIST
(The right half of the directory window)

* Double-click on a directory name's . . . . 📁
  to make current.

  File Manager updates directory contents list.

54

EXPANDING DIRECTORY LEVELS

FROM FILE MANAGER WINDOW

FROM DIRECTORY TREE
(The left half of the directory window)

TO SHOW ALL DIRECTORY LEVELS:

1. Click on . . . . **Tree**

2. Click on . . . . **Expand All**

TO SHOW FIRST-LEVEL SUBDIRECTORIES BELOW CURRENT DIRECTORY:

• Double-click on a directory name's . . . . ☐ in the directory tree.

   NOTE: If the Indicate Expandable Branches option (page 56) is selected, directory icons containing subdirectories are marked with a plus sign (+).

OR

1. Click on a directory name's . . . . ☐ in the directory tree.

2. Click on . . . . **Tree**

3. Click on . . . . **Expand One Level**

TO VIEW ALL SUBDIRECTORIES BELOW CURRENT DIRECTORY:

1. Click on a directory name's . . . . ☐ in the directory tree.

2. Click on . . . . **Tree**

3. Click on . . . . **Expand Branch**

COLLAPSING DIRECTORY LEVELS

NOTE: *The steps below will hide all subdirectories below the selected directory icon in the directory tree.*

FROM FILE MANAGER WINDOW

FROM DIRECTORY TREE
(The left half of the directory window)

1. Double-click on a directory name's .... 🗁 in the directory tree.

   File Manager hides all subdirectories below the selected directory.

   NOTE: If the Indicate Expandable Branches option (page 56) is selected, collapsible directory icons are marked with a minus sign (-).

OR

1. Click on a directory name's .... 🗁 in the directory tree.

2. Click on .... **Tree**

3. Click on .... **Collapse Branch**

   File Manager hides all subdirectories below the selected directory.

INDICATING EXPANDABLE DIRECTORIES

NOTE: When this option is selected (✓), it may take a longer time for File Manager to draw the directory tree.

FROM FILE MANAGER WINDOW

FROM DIRECTORY TREE
(The left half of the directory window)

1. Click on . . . . **Tree**
2. Click on . . . . **Indicate Expandable Branches** to select (✓) or deselect.

    Expandable directory icons contain a plus sign (+), and collapsible directory icons contain a minus (-) sign.

MINIMIZING A DIRECTORY WINDOW

See Minimizing a Window, page 6.

OPENING A DIRECTORY ICON

See Opening a Document Icon, page 20.

CLOSING A DIRECTORY ICON

See Closing a Document Icon, page 21.

CREATING A NEW DIRECTORY WINDOW

FROM FILE MANAGER WINDOW

TO CREATE A NEW WINDOW FOR THE SAME DRIVE:

• Double-click on the current drive icon in the drive list area.

NOTE: The current drive icon is surrounded by a rectangle.

TO CREATE A NEW WINDOW FOR A DIFFERENT DRIVE:

• Double-click on a drive icon in the drive list area.

TO CREATE A NEW WINDOW FOR A DIRECTORY:

FROM DIRECTORY TREE

(The left half of the directory window)

• Press and hold . . . . |Shift|

    and double-click on a directory name's . . . . ⬜

    in the directory tree.

NOTE: File Manager displays a new directory window showing the directory's contents. To display the directory tree in the new window, see Directory Window View Options, page 59.

SELECTING A DIRECTORY WINDOW

FROM FILE MANAGER WINDOW

*   Click anywhere on the directory window.

TO SELECT A <u>HIDDEN</u> DIRECTORY WINDOW:

1. Click on . . . . **<u>W</u>indow**
2. Click on the name of desired directory.

TO MOVE SELECTION QUICKLY AMONG DIRECTORY WINDOWS:

*   Press . . . . **Ctrl** + **Tab**
    until title of desired directory window is highlighted.

CLOSING A DIRECTORY WINDOW

NOTE: If only one directory window is open, it cannot be closed.

FROM FILE MANAGER WINDOW

*   Double-click on directory window's . . . . □

OR

1. Click on directory window's . . . . □
2. Click on . . . . **<u>C</u>lose**

DIRECTORY WINDOW VIEW OPTIONS

NOTE: Changes affect the selected window only.

FROM FILE MANAGER WINDOW

1.   Select desired directory window (page 58).

2.   Click on . . . . **View**

TO VIEW DIRECTORY TREE AND DIRECTORY CONTENTS LIST:

NOTE: This is the default setting.

3.   Click on . . . . **Tree and Directory**
     The directory window shows the directory tree on the left and the contents of the current directory on the right.

OR

TO VIEW DIRECTORY TREE ONLY:

3.   Click on . . . . **Tree Only**

OR

TO VIEW DIRECTORY CONTENTS LIST ONLY:

3.   Click on . . . . **Directory Only**

SPECIFYING DIRECTORY AND FILE INFORMATION TO BE DISPLAYED

NOTE: Changes affect the amount of information displayed in the selected window's directory contents list.

FROM FILE MANAGER WINDOW

1. Select desired directory window (page 58).

2. Click on . . . . **View**

TO SHOW ONLY DIRECTORY AND FILE NAMES:

- Click on . . . . **Name**

OR

TO SHOW ALL FILE INFORMATION:

- Click on . . . . **All File Details**

OR

TO SHOW SPECIFIC FILE INFORMATION:

a) Click on . . . . **Partial Details...**

b) Click on desired options to select (⊠) or deselect (☐):

- . . . . ☐ **Size**

- . . . . ☐ Last **M**odification Date

- . . . . ☐ Last Modification **T**ime

- . . . . ☐ **F**ile Attributes

c) Click on . . . . [**OK**]

SPECIFYING SORT ORDER OF DIRECTORY INFORMATION

NOTE: Changes affect the directory contents list in the selected directory window.

FROM FILE MANAGER WINDOW

1. Select desired directory window (page 58).

2. Click on . . . . **View**

3. Click on one of the following:

    ● . . . . **Sort by Name**
    (Shows directories and files listed alphabetically by their names.)

    ● . . . . **Sort by Type**
    (Shows directories and files listed alphabetically by their extensions.)

    ● . . . . **Sort by Size**
    (Shows files in size order.)

    ● . . . . **Sort by Date**
    (Shows directories and files listed by their last modification date.)

SPECIFYING FILE TYPES TO DISPLAY

NOTE: Changes affect the directory contents list in the selected directory window.

FROM FILE MANAGER WINDOW

1. Select desired directory window (page 58).

2. Click on . . . . **View**

3. Click on . . . . **By File Type...**

   • Type a filespec in . . . . N̲ame: [   ]

   NOTE: The filespec you type works in combination with the options you select below. For example: If you type *.EXE, *you must also select the Programs option to display .EXE (program) files.*

   AND/OR

   • Click on desired options to select (⊠) or deselect (☐):

     ● . . . . ☐ D̲irectories
     (Select to show subdirectories of current directory.)

     ● . . . . ☐ P̲rograms
     (Select to show application files [files with .EXE, .COM, .BAT, or .PIF extensions].)

     ● . . . . ☐ Docume̲nts
     (Select to show associated data files.)

     ● . . . . ☐ O̲ther Files
     (Select to show files not included above.)

     ● . . . . ☐ Show Hidden/S̲ystem Files
     (Select to show system or hidden files.)

4. Click on . . . . [OK]

REFRESHING DIRECTORY INFORMATION

NOTE: File Manager rereads the drive and updates the directory tree and directory contents list.

FROM FILE MANAGER WINDOW

1. Select directory window (page 58) to update.

2. Click on the selected directory window's current drive icon in the drive list area.

    NOTE: The current drive icon is surrounded by a rectangle.

    OR

    a) Click on . . . . **Window**

    b) Click on . . . . **Refresh**

ARRANGING DIRECTORY WINDOWS AND ICONS

See Arranging Document Windows and Icons, page 22.
See Moving a Window or Icon, page 5.

MOVING A DIRECTORY WINDOW'S SPLIT BAR

NOTE: The split bar divides the directory tree and directory contents list.

FROM FILE MANAGER WINDOW

1. Point to split bar.
    Pointer becomes a ←|→ .

2. Click, hold and drag split bar left or right to desired location.

3. Release mouse button.

SHOWING OR HIDING THE STATUS BAR

NOTE: When this option is selected (✓), the status bar appears at the bottom of the File Manager window and shows information about the current drive and directory.

FROM FILE MANAGER WINDOW

1. Click on . . . . **Options**

2. Click on . . . . **Status Bar**
    to select (✓) or deselect.

CHANGING FONT ATTRIBUTES FOR DIRECTORY WINDOWS

FROM FILE MANAGER WINDOW

1. Click on . . . . **Options**

2. Click on . . . . **Font...**

TO CHANGE FONT:

- Click on desired font name in <u>F</u>ont list box.

TO SPECIFY FONT STYLE:

- Click on one of the following in Font St<u>y</u>le list box:

    - . . . . Regular
    - . . . . Italic
    - . . . . Bold
    - . . . . Bold Italic

TO SPECIFY FONT SIZE:

- Click on desired point size in <u>S</u>ize list box.

TO SHOW TEXT IN ALL UPPER CASE:

- Click on . . . . ☒ <u>L</u>owercase to deselect (☐).

3. Click on . . . . [**OK**]

USING FILE MANAGER'S "SAVE SETTINGS ON EXIT" OPTION

NOTE: *When this option is selected (✓), File Manager will save all directory window and icon positions and all selected View menu options as they are when you exit File Manager. Selections from the Options menu are saved automatically and are not influenced by this command.*

FROM FILE MANAGER WINDOW

1. Click on . . . . **Options**

2. Click on . . . . **Save Settings on Exit**
   to select (✓) or deselect.

SAVING CURRENT VIEW AND SETTINGS WITHOUT EXITING FILE MANAGER

NOTE: *File Manager saves all directory window and icon positions and all selected View menu options. Selections from the Options menu are saved automatically and are not influenced by this command.*

FROM FILE MANAGER WINDOW

1. Click on . . . . **File**

2. Press and hold . . . . **Shift**

   and click on . . . . **Exit**

CREATING A DIRECTORY

FROM FILE MANAGER WINDOW

FROM DIRECTORY TREE
(The left half of the directory window)

1. Click on a directory name's . . . . ☐

    below which subdirectory will be created.

    *NOTE: To create a first-level subdirectory, click on the root
    directory icon at the top of the directory tree.*

2. Click on . . . . **File**

3. Click on . . . . **Create Directory...**

4. Type a new directory name in . . <u>N</u>ame: ☐

    EXAMPLE: WPDOC

    *NOTE: To create a directory that is not below the currently
    selected directory, you must type the full pathname.
    For example, type \Level1, where the backslash (\)
    represents the root directory.*

5. Click on . . . . `OK`

SEARCHING FOR FILES AND DIRECTORIES

NOTE: *This procedure creates a "Search Results" window that shows files and directories that have related filenames.*

FROM FILE MANAGER WINDOW

FROM DIRECTORY TREE

(The left half of the directory window)

1. Click on a directory name's .... 📁
   where search will begin.

2. Click on .... **File**

3. Click on .... **Searc̲h...**

4. Type a directory name, filename,
   or filespec in .... Search For: [＿＿＿]

   EXAMPLE: Type *＊.PM4* *(a filespec) to locate files that have a .PM4 filename extension.*

TO SEARCH ONLY THE CURRENT DIRECTORY:

• Click on .... ☒ Se̲arch All Subdirectories
  to deselect (☐).

5. Click on .... [OK]

   File Manager displays a Search Result window containing all found files and directories.

SELECTING FILES AND DIRECTORIES

NOTE: *Select directory items (files and directories) before executing commands such as copy, move and delete.*
The following selection options can be combined to select any combination of directory items.

FROM FILE MANAGER WINDOW

TO SELECT ONE DIRECTORY ITEM:

FROM DIRECTORY TREE OR DIRECTORY CONTENTS LIST

• Click on desired directory item.

TO SELECT TWO OR MORE DIRECTORY ITEMS IN SEQUENCE:

FROM DIRECTORY CONTENTS LIST
(The right half of the directory window)

1. Click on first directory item.

2. Press . . . . ⏍**Shift**
   <u>and</u> click on last directory item in group to select.

TO SELECT NON-CONSECUTIVE DIRECTORY ITEMS:

FROM DIRECTORY CONTENTS LIST
(The right half of the directory window)

• Press . . . . ⏍**Ctrl**
  <u>and</u> click on each directory item.

TO DESELECT INDIVIDUAL DIRECTORY ITEMS:

• Press . . . . ⏍**Ctrl**
  <u>and</u> click on each directory item to deselect.

TO DESELECT A MULTIPLE SELECTION OF DIRECTORY ITEMS:

• Click on any directory item.

USING FILENAME PATTERNS TO SELECT OR DESELECT GROUPS OF FILES

FROM FILE MANAGER WINDOW

FROM DIRECTORY CONTENTS LIST
(The right half of the directory window)

1. Click on . . . . **File**

2. Click on . . . . **Select Files...**

3. Type a filespec in . . . . <u>F</u>ile(s): [   ]

   EXAMPLE: Type <u>.TXT</u> to select/deselect all files with a .TXT filename extension.*

4. Click on . . . . [<u>S</u>elect]

   to select files specified in Files text box.

   OR

   Click on . . . . [<u>D</u>eselect]

   to deselect files specified in Files text box.

5. Repeat steps 3 and 4 until all desired files are selected or deselected.

6. Click on . . . . [<u>C</u>lose]

MOVING FILES AND DIRECTORIES
— Using the Mouse

NOTE: *Selected directory items (files and directories) can be*
moved from one directory window (the source window) to
another directory window (the destination window), or to a
directory or drive icon (the destination icon).

If the destination is a diskette drive, insert diskette before
moving directory items.

Files cannot be renamed when moved with a mouse. See
Moving Files and Directories — Using the Menu, page 73.

FROM FILE MANAGER WINDOW

1. If necessary, arrange source window and destination
    window or icon so that both are in view (page 22).

2. Select directory item(s) to move.

    See Selecting Files and Directories, page 69.

    NOTE: If you select a directory, all its files and subdirectories
    will be moved.

**TO MOVE DIRECTORY ITEMS TO A DESTINATION WINDOW
OR ICON ON THE SAME DRIVE:**

a) Click, hold and drag directory item(s) onto
    destination window or icon.

    Pointer becomes a ▯ when placed on destination window
    or icon.

b) Release mouse button.

Continued ...

MOVING FILES AND DIRECTORIES
— **Using the Mouse (continued)**

**TO MOVE DIRECTORY ITEMS TO A DESTINATION WINDOW
OR ICON ON A DIFFERENT DRIVE:**

    a) Press . . . . **Shift**

       <u>and</u> click, hold and drag directory item(s)
       onto destination window or icon.

       Pointer becomes a ⬜ *when placed on destination window
       or icon.*

       *NOTE: If a file is moved to a drive icon, the file is placed
             in the current directory of that drive.*

    b) Release mouse button and key.

3. Click on . . . . **Yes**
    to confirm move.

MOVING FILES AND DIRECTORIES
— Using the Menu

*NOTE: These steps allow you to rename files or a directory
during the move.*

FROM FILE MANAGER WINDOW

FROM DIRECTORY TREE OR DIRECTORY CONTENTS LIST

1. Select directory or file(s) to move.
    See Selecting Files and Directories, page 69.

    *NOTE: If you select a directory, all its files and subdirectories
    will be moved.*

2. Click on . . . . **File**

3. Click on . . . . **Move...**

4. Type a destination directory
    and/or a filename in . . . . <u>T</u>o: [   ]

    *NOTE: You can substitute a filespec for a filename to rename
    multiple files during the move. EXAMPLE: Type
    \NEWDIR*.DOC to move selected files to the NEWDIR
    directory and change all extensions of moved files
    to .DOC.*

5. Click on . . . . [OK]

COPYING FILES AND DIRECTORIES
— Using the Mouse

*NOTE: Selected directory items (files and directories) can be
copied from one directory window (the source window) to
another directory window (the destination window), or to a
directory or drive icon (the destination icon).
If the destination is a diskette drive, insert diskette
before copying.*

FROM FILE MANAGER WINDOW

1. Arrange source window and destination window or
    icon so that both are in view (page 22).

2. Select directory item(s) to copy.

    See Selecting Files and Directories, page 69.

    *NOTE: If you select a directory, all its files and subdirectories
    will be copied.*

**TO COPY DIRECTORY ITEMS TO A DESTINATION WINDOW
OR ICON ON A DIFFERENT DRIVE:**

   a) Click, hold and drag directory item(s) onto
       destination window or icon.

       Pointer becomes a 🔲 *when placed on destination window
       or icon.*

   b) Release mouse button.

Continued ...

COPYING FILES AND DIRECTORIES
— **Using the Mouse (continued)**

TO COPY DIRECTORY ITEMS TO A DESTINATION WINDOW OR ICON ON THE SAME DRIVE:

   a) Press . . . . `Ctrl`

     <u>and</u> click, hold and drag directory item(s) onto destination window or icon.

     Pointer becomes a ▨ when placed on destination window or icon.

     NOTE: If a file is copied to a drive icon, the file is placed in the current directory of that drive.

   b) Release mouse button and key.

3. Click on . . . . `Yes` to confirm copy.

COPYING FILES AND DIRECTORIES
— Using the Menu

*NOTE: These steps allow you to rename files or a directory
during the copy.*

FROM FILE MANAGER WINDOW

FROM DIRECTORY TREE OR DIRECTORY CONTENTS LIST

1. Select directory or file(s) to copy.
    See Selecting Files and Directories, page 69.

    *NOTE: If you select a directory, all its files and subdirectories
    will be copied.*

2. Click on . . . . **File**

3. Click on . . . . **Copy...**

4. Type a destination path
    and/or a filename in . . . . **To:** [   ]

    *NOTE: You can substitute a filespec for a filename to rename
    multiple files during the copy. EXAMPLE: Type
    \DUPLICATES*.DOC to copy selected files to the
    DUPLICATES directory and change all extensions of
    copied files to .DOC.*

5. Click on . . . . OK

DELETING FILES AND DIRECTORIES

NOTE: <u>*CAUTION*</u>: *When a directory is deleted, all of its files and subdirectories are erased from the disk.*

FROM FILE MANAGER WINDOW

FROM DIRECTORY TREE OR DIRECTORY CONTENTS LIST

1. Select directory(s) or file(s) to delete.
   See Selecting Files and Directories, page 69.

2. Click on . . . . **File**

3. Click on . . . . **Delete**

4. Click on . . . . [**OK**]

5. Click on . . . . [**Yes**]
   to confirm deletion of each selected file or directory.

   OR

   Click on . . . . [**Yes To All**]
   to delete all selected files without confirmation.

RENAMING A FILE OR DIRECTORY

NOTE: <u>*CAUTION*</u>:   *Do not rename files or directories related to the Windows program itself.*

FROM FILE MANAGER WINDOW

FROM DIRECTORY TREE OR DIRECTORY CONTENTS LIST

1. Select directory or file to rename.
    See Selecting Files and Directories, page 69.

2. Click on . . . . **File**

3. Click on . . . . **Rename...**

4. Click in . . . . **To:** [   ]

5. Type a new name.

6. Click on . . . . [**OK**]

RENAMING A GROUP OF FILES

NOTE: <u>*CAUTION:*</u> *Do not rename files related to the*
Windows program itself.

FROM FILE MANAGER WINDOW

1. Select directory containing files to rename.
   See Changing the Current Directory, page 53.

FROM DIRECTORY CONTENTS LIST
(The right half of the directory window)

2. Select files to rename.
   See Selecting Files and Directories, page 69.

3. Click on . . . . **File**

4. Click on . . . . **Re̲name...**

**TO USE A FILENAME PATTERN TO SPECIFY FILES
TO RENAME:**

   a) Click, hold and drag mouse through
      text to replace in . . . . F̲rom: ☐

   b) Type a filespec for file group to be renamed.
      *EXAMPLE: *.OLD*

5. Click in . . . . T̲o: ☐

6. Type a filespec specifying new names.
   *EXAMPLE: *.NEW*

7. Click on . . . . [OK]

CHANGING FILE ATTRIBUTES

NOTE: A file attribute indicates how a file can be used.

FROM FILE MANAGER WINDOW

1.   Select directory containing file to change.
     See Changing the Current Directory, page 53.

FROM DIRECTORY CONTENTS LIST
(The right half of the directory window)

2.   Click on file to change.

3.   Click on . . . . **File**

4.   Click on . . . . **Properties...**

5.   Click on one or more options to select (☒)
     or deselect (☐):

     ● . . . . ☐ Read Only
     (Select to prevent modification of file.)

     ● . . . . ☐ Archive
     (Select to show file has been modified.)

     ● . . . . ☐ Hidden
     (Select to hide file in an MS-DOS directory listing.)

     ● . . . . ☐ System
     (Select to identify file as MS-DOS system file.)

6.   Click on . . . . OK

ASSOCIATING DATA FILES WITH APPLICATIONS

NOTE: *This procedure associates filename extensions with a specific application. This allows File Manager to start the application and open a data file in one step.*

FROM FILE MANAGER WINDOW

1. Select directory containing file to associate.
   See Changing the Current Directory, page 53.

FROM DIRECTORY CONTENTS LIST
(The right half of the directory window)

2. Click on any data file that has the filename extension you want to associate with an application.

3. Click on . . . . **File**

4. Click on . . . . **Associate...**

5. Click on application name to associate with the extension in the <u>A</u>ssociate With list box.

   IF the application is not listed,

   a) Click on . . . . | **Browse...** |

   b) Double-click on desired application name in File <u>N</u>ame list box.
      See Locating Files, page 10.

TO REMOVE AN ASSOCIATION:

   • Click on . . . . (None)
     in the <u>A</u>ssociate With list box.

6. Click on . . . . | **OK** |

FORMATTING DISKETTES

FROM FILE MANAGER WINDOW

1. Insert diskette to format in disk drive.

2. Click on . . . . **Disk**

3. Click on . . . . **Format Disk...**

4. Click on . . . . **Disk In:** [↓]

5. Click on disk drive containing diskette to format.

6. Click on . . . . **Capacity:** [↓]

7. Click on size of diskette to format.

TO LABEL DISKETTE:

   a) Click in . . . . **Label:** [ ]

   b) Type a label name.

TO INCLUDE SYSTEM FILES:

   • Click on . . . . [ ] **Make** System Disk
     to select (⊠).

TO QUICKLY FORMAT A PREVIOUSLY FORMATTED DISKETTE:

   • Click on . . . . [ ] **Quick** Format
     to select (⊠).

NOTE: When this option is selected, the root directory and file allocation table on the formatted diskette are deleted. The diskette is not scanned for errors.

8. Click on . . . . [**OK**]

9. Click on . . . . [**Yes**]

MAKING A SYSTEM DISKETTE

FROM FILE MANAGER WINDOW

1. Insert a formatted diskette to receive system files in disk drive.

2. Click on . . . . **Disk**

3. Click on . . . . **Make System Disk...**

IF system contains two diskette drives,

   a) Click on . . . . Copy System Files to Disk: ⬇

   b) Click on letter of disk drive containing diskette to receive system files.

   c) Click on . . . . `OK`

COPYING A DISKETTE USING A SINGLE DISK DRIVE SYSTEM

NOTE: *The source and destination diskettes must be of the same type and capacity.*

FROM FILE MANAGER WINDOW

1. Insert source diskette with files to copy in disk drive.

2. Click on . . . . **Disk**

3. Click on . . . . **Copy Disk...**

4. Click on . . . . **Yes**
   to confirm.

5. When prompted, insert diskette to receive files in disk drive.

6. Replace the source and destination diskettes as directed during the copy process.

COPYING A DISKETTE USING A DUAL DISK DRIVE SYSTEM

NOTE: The source and destination diskettes must be of the same type and capacity.

FROM FILE MANAGER WINDOW

1. Insert source diskette with files to copy in source disk drive.

IF   your system has two diskette drives of the <u>same size</u>,

   - Insert a diskette to receive information in destination disk drive.

2. Click on . . . . **Disk**

3. Click on . . . . **Copy Disk...**

4. Click on . . . . **Source In:** ⬇

5. Click on letter of source disk drive.

6. Click on . . . . **Destination In:** ⬇

7. Click on letter of destination disk drive.

8. Click on . . . . [**OK**]

9. Click on . . . . [**Yes**]
   to confirm.

CREATING OR CHANGING A LABEL FOR A DISK

FROM FILE MANAGER WINDOW

IF labeling a diskette,

1. • Insert diskette to label in disk drive.

   • Click on diskette's . . . .
   then execute step 2.

OR

IF labeling a hard disk,

1. • Click on . . . .
   to label in drive area.

2. Click on . . . . **Disk**

3. Click on . . . . **Label Disk**

4. Click in . . . . <u>L</u>abel:

5. Type a label.

6. Click on . . . .   OK

PRINTING ASSOCIATED DATA FILES FROM FILE MANAGER

NOTE: *See Associating Data Files with Applications, page 81.*
Not all applications support this procedure.

FROM FILE MANAGER WINDOW

TO PRINT A FILE USING THE PRINT COMMAND:

1. Select directory containing file to print.
   See Changing the Current Directory, page 53.

FROM DIRECTORY CONTENTS LIST
(The right half of the directory window)

2. Click on an associated file's . . . . ▤

3. Click on . . . . **File**

4. Click on . . . . **Print...**

5. Click on . . . . [OK]

TO PRINT A FILE BY DRAGGING IT ONTO PRINT MANAGER:

1. If necessary, run Print Manager (page 95) and reduce it to an icon.

2. Select directory containing file to print.
   See Changing the Current Directory, page 53.

FROM DIRECTORY CONTENTS LIST
(The right half of the directory window)

3. Click, hold and drag an associated file's . . . . ▤

   onto . . . .

   Print Manager

4. Release mouse button.

STARTING AN APPLICATION FROM FILE MANAGER

See Running an Application Using the Run Command, page 14.
See Running an Application Using File Icons, page 15.

MINIMIZING OR RETAINING FILE MANAGER'S WINDOW WHEN RUNNING AN APPLICATION

NOTE: *When this option is selected (✓), File Manager will run as an icon whenever an application is started from File Manager. The File Manager icon will be placed on the bottom of the desktop (the area below all windows).*

FROM FILE MANAGER WINDOW

1. Click on . . . . **Options**

2. Click on . . . . **Minimize on Use**
   to select (✓) or deselect.

TURNING DISPLAY OF CONFIRMATION MESSAGES ON OR OFF

NOTE: <u>*CAUTION:*</u> *These messages provide important safeguards against performing unwanted actions that can result in a loss of data.*

FROM FILE MANAGER WINDOW

1. Click on . . . . **Options**

2. Click on . . . . **Confirmation...**

3. Click on desired options to select (☒)
   or deselect (☐):

   • . . . . ☒ File Delete
   (Deselect to remove warning message before files are deleted.)

   • . . . . ☒ Directory Delete
   (Deselect to remove warning message before directories are deleted.)

   • . . . . ☒ File Replace
   (Deselect to remove warning message before overwriting an existing file.)

   • . . . . ☒ Mouse Action
   (Deselect to remove warning message before moving or copying files by dragging them with a mouse.)

   • . . . . ☒ Disk Commands
   (Deselect to remove warning message before formatting or copying a diskette.)

4. Click on . . . . OK

CONNECTING TO A NETWORK DISK DRIVE

FROM FILE MANAGER WINDOW

NOTE: *To use File Manager network options, start the network before starting Windows.*

1. Click on . . . . **Disk**

2. Click on . . . . **Network Connections...**

   OR

   Click on . . . . **Connect Network Drive...**

FROM NETWORK CONNECTIONS DIALOG BOX

NOTE: *The steps below will vary depending upon the* <u>*type of network installed*</u> *and the options displayed.*

3. Click in . . . . <u>N</u>etwork Path: [   ]

4. Type the network pathname.

NOTE: *Some networks allow users to browse through and select a drive.*

TO CHANGE PROPOSED NETWORK DRIVE:

   a) Click on . . . . D<u>r</u>ive: ⬇

   b) Click on desired drive letter.

TO ENTER A PASSWORD:

   a) Click in . . . . Pass<u>w</u>ord: [   ]

   b) Type the password.

Continued ...

CONNECTING TO A NETWORK DISK DRIVE
(continued)

5. Click on . . . . `Connect`
   to save the settings and automatically
   connect the next time Windows is started.

   OR

   Press and hold . . . . `Shift`

   __and__ click on . . . . `Connect`

   to limit connection to current work session.

TO CONNECT TO ANOTHER NETWORK DRIVE:

   • Execute steps 3-5 for each network drive.

6. Click on . . . . `Close`

CONNECTING TO AN ESTABLISHED NETWORK DISK DRIVE

FROM FILE MANAGER WINDOW

*NOTE: To use File Manager network options, start the
         network before starting Windows.*

1. Click on . . . . **Disk**

2. Click on . . . . **Network Connections...**

    OR

    Click on . . . . **Connect Network Drive...**

FROM NETWORK CONNECTIONS DIALOG BOX

*NOTE: The steps below will vary depending upon the <u>type of
         network installed</u> and the options displayed.*

3. Click on . . . . `Previous`

4. Click on desired network path.

5. Click on . . . . `Select`

TO ENTER A PASSWORD:

    a) Click in . . . . Pass<u>w</u>ord: ▢

    b) Type the password.

6. Click on . . . . `Connect`

7. Click on . . . . `Close`

DISCONNECTING FROM NETWORK DISK DRIVES

FROM FILE MANAGER WINDOW

NOTE: *To use File Manager network options, start the*
network before starting Windows.
If you are running Windows in 386 enhanced mode, you
may not be able to disconnect from network drives that
were active before you started Windows.

1. Click on . . . . **Disk**

2. Click on . . . . **Network Connections...**

   OR

   Click on . . . . **Disconnect Network Drive...**

FROM NETWORK CONNECTIONS DIALOG BOX

NOTE: *The steps below will vary depending upon the type of*
network installed and the options displayed.

3. Click on network drive to disconnect in Current Drive
   Connections list box.

4. Click on . . . . `Disconnect`

5. Click on . . . . `Close`

ADDING A NEW PROGRAM ITEM TO A PROGRAM MANAGER GROUP USING FILE MANAGER

FROM FILE MANAGER WINDOW

1. Select directory containing application or associated data file to add to a group.
   See Changing the Current Directory, page 53.

2. Arrange desktop so that File Manager's directory contents list and the destination group in Program Manager are both in view.

FROM FILE MANAGER DIRECTORY CONTENTS LIST
(The right half of the directory window)

3. Click, hold and drag an application file's . . .

   OR

   Click hold and drag an associated file's . . . . . .

   onto the destination group.
   Pointer becomes a ⬚ when placed on destination group.

4. Release mouse button.

QUITTING FILE MANAGER

See Closing an Application Window or Icon, page 23.
Also see Using File Manager's "Save Settings on Exit"
Option, page 66.

MAKING PRINT MANAGER ACTIVE

NOTE: When Print Manager is active (the default setting), it will automatically run as an icon on the bottom of the desktop when you print from any Windows application.

FROM PROGRAM MANAGER MAIN GROUP WINDOW

1. Double-click on . . . .

Control Panel

FROM CONTROL PANEL WINDOW

2. Double-click on . . . .

Printers

3. Click on . . . . ☐ Use Print Manager to select (☒).

4. Click on . . . . Close

RUNNING PRINT MANAGER MANUALLY

NOTE: You can run Print Manager manually to make certain changes to the print settings before sending files to the printer.
Requires that Print Manager is active (see above).

FROM PROGRAM MANAGER MAIN GROUP WINDOW

• Double-click on . . . .

Print Manager

Print Manager window appears, displaying installed printers.

VIEWING PRINT JOBS SENT TO PRINT MANAGER

*NOTE: Requires that Print Manager is active (page 95) and that
files have been sent to a printer.*

TO OPEN PRINT MANAGER AND VIEW A LOCAL PRINT QUEUE:

*   Double-click on . . . .

    on the bottom of the desktop.

OR

1.   Click on any application window's . . . .

2.   Click on . . . . **S<u>w</u>itch To...**

3.   Click on Print Manager name in Task List.

*Print Manager window appears, displaying installed printers and
a list of print files (called a queue).*

TO OPEN PRINT MANAGER AND VIEW A NETWORK PRINT QUEUE:

FROM PROGRAM MANAGER MAIN GROUP WINDOW

*   Double-click on . . . .

*Print Manager window appears, displaying installed
printers and a list of print files (called a queue).*

*NOTE: The files listed under network printers are only
those you sent to the network printer. To see all
files sent to a network printer, see Viewing Entire
Network Print Queue for a Connected Printer,
page 105.*

CANCELING PRINT JOBS SENT TO PRINT MANAGER

NOTE: Not all networks support this option.

1. Open Print Manager.
   See Viewing Print Jobs Sent to Print Manager, page 96.

FROM PRINT MANAGER WINDOW

TO CANCEL A SINGLE PRINT JOB:

2. Click on print file to cancel in the queue.

3. Click on . . . . `Delete`

4. Click on . . . . `OK`

TO CANCEL ALL PRINT JOBS:

2. Click on . . . . **View**

3. Click on . . . . **Exit**

4. Click on . . . . `OK`

NOTE: If a file currently printing is canceled, the printer may have to be reset to clear its memory.

CLOSING PRINT MANAGER

NOTE: If Print Manager is running as an icon, it automatically closes when all print files in a local queue have been printed. Use the following procedure when Print Manager is running in a window.

FROM PRINT MANAGER WINDOW

1. Click on . . . . **View**

2. Click on . . . . **Exit**

PAUSING AND RESUMING A PRINT JOB SENT TO PRINT MANAGER

NOTE: Not all networks support this option.

1. Open Print Manager.
    See Viewing Print Jobs Sent to Print Manager, page 96.

FROM PRINT MANAGER WINDOW

TO PAUSE CURRENT PRINT JOB:

2. Click on print file to pause in the queue.

3. Click on . . . .   [**Pause**]

TO RESUME PRINTING:

2. Click on print file that has been paused.

3. Click on . . . .   [**Resume**]

CHANGING ORDER OF FILES TO PRINT IN A PRINT QUEUE

*NOTE: The order of print files in a <u>network</u> print queue
             cannot be changed.*

1. Open Print Manager.

    See Viewing Print Jobs Sent to Print Manager, page 96.

FROM PRINT MANAGER WINDOW

2. Point to name of file to move in the print queue.

    *NOTE: The first print file or the file currently printing
                cannot be moved.*

3. Click, hold and drag file to new position in queue.

4. Release mouse button.

100

HIDE OR DISPLAY TIME AND DATE OF PRINT FILES IN A PRINT QUEUE

*NOTE: By default, the option below is selected (✓). Deselect
the option to hide the time and date of print files.*

1. Open Print Manager.
    See Viewing Print Jobs Sent to Print Manager, page 96.
    See Running Print Manager Manually, page 95.

FROM PRINT MANAGER WINDOW

2. Click on . . . . **View**

3. Click on . . . . **Time/Date Sent**
    to select (✓) or deselect.

HIDE OR DISPLAY SIZE OF PRINT FILES IN A PRINT QUEUE

*NOTE: By default, the option below is selected (✓). Deselect
the option to hide the size of print files.*

1. Open Print Manager.
    See Viewing Print Jobs Sent to Print Manager, page 96.
    See Running Print Manager Manually, page 95.

FROM PRINT MANAGER WINDOW

2. Click on . . . . **View**

3. Click on . . . . **Print File Size**
    to select (✓) or deselect.

SETTING PRINT SPEED WHEN USING PRINT MANAGER

1. Open Print Manager.

   See Viewing Print Jobs Sent to Print Manager, page 96.
   See Running Print Manager Manually, page 95.

FROM PRINT MANAGER WINDOW

2. Click on . . . . **Options**

3. Click on one of the following to select:

   NOTE: A check mark (✓) before the option name
   indicates that it has been selected.

   ● . . . . **Low Priority**
   (Decreases printing speed.)

   ● . . . . **Medium Priority**
   (Sets the default printing speed.)

   ● . . . . **High Priority**
   (Increases printing speed.)

DISPLAYING PRINT MANAGER MESSAGES

1. Open Print Manager.

    See Viewing Print Jobs Sent to Print Manager, page 96.
    See Running Print Manager Manually, page 95.

FROM PRINT MANAGER WINDOW

2. Click on . . . . **Options**

3. Click on one of the following to select:

    *NOTE: A check mark (✓) before the option name
              indicates that it has been selected.*

    ● . . . . **Alert Always**

    *(Displays messages when interaction
    with Print Manager is required.)*

    ● . . . . **Flash if Inactive**

    *(Flashes Print Manager icon or Print
    Manager window's title bar when interaction
    with Print Manager is required.)*

    NOTE: This is the default setting.

    ● . . . .**Ignore if Inactive**

    *(Excludes message when interaction
    with Print Manager is required.)*

USING PRINT MANAGER TO CONNECT TO A NETWORK PRINTER

1. Open Print Manager.

   See Viewing Print Jobs Sent to Print Manager, page 96.
   See Running Print Manager Manually, page 95.

FROM PRINT MANAGER WINDOW

2. Click on . . . . **Options**

3. Click on . . . . **Network Connections...**

FROM PRINTERS — NETWORK CONNECTIONS DIALOG BOX

NOTE: The steps below will vary depending upon the <u>type of</u>
<u>network installed</u> and the options displayed.

4. Click in . . . . Network Path: [   ]

5. Type your network name.

   NOTE: Consult your network documentation.

6. Click on . . . . Port: ⬇

7. Click on port to connect to.

TO ENTER PASSWORD:

   a) Click in . . . . Password: [   ]

   b) Type your required password.
      An asterisk appears for each character typed.

8. Click on . . . . [**Connect**]

   Printer is added to printer list.

9. Click on . . . . [**Close**]

   The Connect dialog box appears with path for
   network printer displayed next to the port.

10. Click on . . . . [**OK**]

11. Click on . . . . [**Close**]

104

USING PRINT MANAGER TO RECONNECT TO A NETWORK PRINTER

NOTE: Not all networks support this option.

1. Open Print Manager.
    See Viewing Print Jobs Sent to Print Manager, page 96.
    See Running Print Manager Manually, page 95.

FROM PRINT MANAGER WINDOW

2. Click on . . . . **Options**

3. Click on . . . . **Network Connections...**

FROM PRINTERS — NETWORK CONNECTIONS DIALOG BOX

*NOTE: The steps below will vary depending upon the <u>type of</u>
        <u>network installed</u> and the options displayed.*

4. Click on . . . . `Previous`

5. Click on network path for printer to reconnect to in
    Network Paths list box.

6. Click on . . . . `Select`

7. Click on . . . . Po<u>r</u>t: ⬇

8. Click on port to connect to.

TO ENTER PASSWORD:

    a) Click in . . . . Pass<u>w</u>ord: ⬚

    b) Type your required password.
    An asterisk appears for each character typed.

9. Click on . . . . `Connect`

10. Click on . . . . `Close`

DISCONNECTING FROM A NETWORK PRINTER

1. Open Print Manager.

    See Viewing Print Jobs Sent to Print Manager, page 96.
    See Running Print Manager Manually, page 95.

FROM PRINT MANAGER WINDOW

2. Click on . . . . **Options**

3. Click on . . . . **Network Connections...**

4. Click on network printer to disconnect in Current Printer Connections list box.

5. Click on . . . . | **Disconnect** |

6. Click on . . . . | **Close** |

VIEWING ENTIRE NETWORK PRINT QUEUE FOR A CONNECTED PRINTER

1. Open Print Manager.

    See Viewing Print Jobs Sent to Print Manager, page 96.
    See Running Print Manager Manually, page 95.

FROM PRINT MANAGER WINDOW

2. Click on a connected network printer.

3. Click on . . . . **View**

4. Click on . . . . **Selected Net Queue...**

5. Click on . . . . | **Close** |

VIEWING NETWORK PRINT QUEUES FOR UNCONNECTED PRINTERS

1. Open Print Manager.

    See Viewing Print Jobs Sent to Print Manager, page 96.
    See Running Print Manager Manually, page 95.

FROM PRINT MANAGER WINDOW

2. Click on . . . . **View**

3. Click on . . . . **Other Net Queue...**

4. Click in . . . . Network Queue: [   ]

5. Type path to network printer for which to show queue.

    NOTE: Consult your network documentation.

6. Click on . . . . [**View**]

    Print Manager displays selected network printer information.

7. Click on . . . . [**Close**]

TURNING OFF AUTOMATIC UPDATE OF A NETWORK PRINT QUEUE

NOTE: *The network queue is automatically updated only when the Print Manager window is open. To speed up network printing, you may want to turn off the automatic update option.*

1. Open Print Manager.

    See Viewing Print Jobs Sent to Print Manager, page 96.
    See Running Print Manager Manually, page 95.

FROM PRINT MANAGER WINDOW

2. Click on . . . . **Options**

3. Click on . . . . **Network Settings...**

4. Click on . . . . ☒ Update Network Display
    to deselect (☐).

5. Click on . . . . ▓▓▓▓▓▓▓
                                                        OK

UPDATING A NETWORK PRINT QUEUE MANUALLY

1. Open Print Manager.

    See Viewing Print Jobs Sent to Print Manager, page 96.
    See Running Print Manager Manually, page 95.

FROM PRINT MANAGER WINDOW

2. Click on . . . . **View**

3. Click on . . . . **Refresh**

108

ROUTING NETWORK FILES THROUGH PRINT MANAGER

NOTE: *Deselect the "Print Net Jobs Direct" option below to give Print Manager control of network print files.*

1. Open Print Manager.

   See Viewing Print Jobs Sent to Print Manager, page 96.
   See Running Print Manager Manually, page 95.

FROM PRINT MANAGER WINDOW

2. Click on . . . . **Options**

3. Click on . . . . **Network Settings...**

4. Click on . . . . ☒ **Print Net Jobs Direct** to deselect (☐).

   NOTE: *When this option is deselected, network printing will take longer because print files will have to pass through both the Print Manager and the network queues.*

5. Click on . . . . `OK`

PRINTING TO FILE USING PRINT MANAGER

1. Open Print Manager.

   See Viewing Print Jobs Sent to Print Manager, page 96.
   See Running Print Manager Manually, page 95.

FROM PRINT MANAGER WINDOW

2. Click on . . . . **Options**

3. Click on . . . . **Printer Setup...**

4. Click on name of destination printer in Installed Printers list box.

5. Click on . . . . **Connect...**

6. Click on "FILE:" option in Ports list box.

7. Click on . . . . **OK**

8. Click on . . . . **Close**

9. Follow your application's printing procedures.

110

SETTING UP PRINTERS
– From Print Manager or Control Panel

See Viewing Print Jobs Sent to Print Manager, page 96.
See Running Print Manager Manually, page 95.
See Opening the Control Panel, page 127.

FROM PRINT MANAGER WINDOW

1. • Click on . . . . **Options**

   • Click on . . . . **Printer Setup...**

OR

FROM CONTROL PANEL WINDOW

1. • Double-click on . . . .

   Printers

TO BYPASS USE OF PRINT MANAGER:

NOTE: This option is only available from the Control Panel –
Printers option.

   • Click on . . . . ☒ Use Print Manager
     to deselect (☐).

TO CHANGE DEFAULT PRINTER:

   a) Click on a printer in Installed Printers list box.

   b) Click on . . . . `Set As Default Printer`

Continued ...

SETTING UP PRINTERS (continued)

TO INSTALL A NEW PRINTER:

a) Click on . . . . [Add >>]

b) Click on a printer in List of Printers list box.

c) Click on . . . . [Install...]

d) If necessary, insert disk containing printer driver files in disk drive.

e) If necessary, type drive and pathname in text box.

f) Click on . . . . [OK]

NOTE: In order to use the printer, it may be necessary to change the port assignment.

TO SELECT A PRINTER PORT:

a) Click on a printer in Installed Printers list box.

b) Click on . . . . [Connect...]

c) Click on a port in Ports list box.

IF a COM port is selected, it may be necessary to change its settings:

• Click on . . . . [Settings...]

See Configuring a Communication Port, page 132, steps b and c.

IF a network port is selected,

• Click on . . . . [Network...]

See Using Print Manager to Connect to a Network Printer, page 103, steps 4-9.

d) Click on . . . . [OK]

Continued ...

112

SETTING UP PRINTERS (continued)

TO PRINT TO A FILE:

a) Click on name of destination printer in Installed Printers list box.

b) Click on . . . . `Connect...`

c) Click on "FILE:" in Ports list box.

d) Click on . . . . `OK`

TO DIRECT PRINTING THROUGH MS-DOS:

NOTE: Print through MS-DOS when using network printers not supported by Windows or when using software that relies on MS-DOS interrupts.

a) Click on a printer in Installed Printers list box.

b) Click on . . . . `Connect...`

c) Click on . . . . . . ☒ Fast Printing Direct to Port to deselect (☐).

d) Click on . . . . `OK`

TO CHANGE PRINTER TIMEOUTS OPTIONS:

a) Click on a printer in Installed Printers list box.

b) Click on . . . . `Connect...`

c) Double-click in. . Device Not Selected: ☐

d) Type a number.

Number represents number of seconds before an off-line message appears.

e) Double-click in. . . Transmission Retry: ☐

Continued ...

SETTING UP PRINTERS (continued)

f) Type a number.

Number represents number of seconds before an information overload message appears.

g) Click on . . . . | OK |

TO REMOVE A PRINTER FROM INSTALLED LIST:

a) Click on a printer in Installed Printers list box.

b) Click on . . . . | Remove |

c) Click on . . . . | Yes |

TO SET PRINTER OPTIONS:

Depending upon your printer, options may include Paper Source, Paper Size (letter, legal, envelope...), Memory, Orientation — Portrait/Landscape, Print Resolution, Cartridges, and Copies.

a) Click on a printer in Installed Printers list box.

b) Click on . . . . | Setup... |

c) Select from available options.

See Selecting Options in a Dialog box, page 8.

TO SET UP FONTS FOR A PRINTER:

a) Click on a printer in Installed Printers list box.

b) Click on . . . . | Setup... |

TO SPECIFY A FONT CARTRIDGE:

1) Click on a cartridge in the Cartridges list box.

TO ADD SOFT FONTS FOR A PRINTER:

1) Click on . . . . | Fonts... |

2) Click on . . . . | Add Fonts... |

Continued ...

114

3) If necessary, type pathname of font files.

4) Click on . . . . `OK`

5) Click on each font to be added from Source list box.

6) Click on . . . . `Add...`

7) Click on . . . . `OK`

TO EDIT FONTS FOR A PRINTER:

1) Click on a font in Printer font list box.

2) Click on . . . . `Edit...`

3) Make changes that apply to selected font.

4) Click on . . . . `OK`

TO CHOOSE A DOWNLOADING PREFERENCE:

1) Click on a font in Printer font list box.

2) Click on . . . . $\bigcirc$ Permanent

OR

Click on . . . . $\bigcirc$ Temporary
to select ($\odot$).

TO COPY INSTALLED FONTS TO ANOTHER PRINTER:

1) Click on desired font(s) in Printer font list box.

2) Click on . . . . `Copy Fonts to New Port...`

3) Click on . . . . `OK`

c) Click on . . . . `Exit`

2. Click on . . . . `Close`

STARTING RECORDER

FROM PROGRAM MANAGER ACCESSORIES
GROUP WINDOW

- Double-click on . . . .

Recorder

RECORDING A MACRO

IF Macro is to be used in a specific application,

- Start application in which macro will be recorded.

1. Run or select Recorder.

FROM RECORDER WINDOW

2. Click on . . . . **Macro**

3. Click on . . . . **Record...**

4. Type name of
   macro in . . . . Record Macro **N**ame: [   ]

5. • Click in . . . . Shortcut **K**ey: [   ]

   • Type letter of <u>second</u> part of shortcut key.

   OR

   • Click on . . . . Shortcut **K**ey: ⬇

   • Click on <u>second</u> part of shortcut key.

Continued ...

RECORDING A MACRO (continued)

6. Click on desired key(s) to select ($\boxtimes$)
    or deselect ($\square$) <u>first</u> part of shortcut key:

*   . . . . $\boxtimes$ Ctrl
*   . . . . $\square$ Shift
*   . . . . $\square$ Alt

> *NOTE: Steps 5 and 6 are used to create a single-combination keystroke (i.e., Ctrl + T). At least one first key should be selected to avoid a conflict with use of your application.*

TO CHANGE LOCATION OF MACRO PLAYBACK:

a) Click on . . . . <u>P</u>layback To: ⬇

b) Click on . . . . Same Application

OR

Click on . . . . Any Application

TO CHANGE SPEED OF MACRO PLAYBACK:

a) Click on . . . . <u>P</u>layback Speed: ⬇

b) Click on . . . . Fast

OR

Click on . . . . Recorded Speed

TO SET MACRO TO RUN CONTINUOUSLY:

*   Click on . . . . $\square$ Continuous Loop
    to select ($\boxtimes$).

TO PREVENT NESTING ONE MACRO WITHIN ANOTHER:

*   Click on . . . . $\boxtimes$ Enable Shortcut Keys
    to deselect ($\square$).

Continued ...

RECORDING A MACRO (continued)

TO SET MOUSE ACTIONS TO BE RECORDED:

NOTE: Recording keystrokes is generally more reliable than recording mouse actions.

   a) Click on . . . . Record Mouse: ⬇

   b) Click on one of the following:

     ● . . . . Ignore Mouse

     ● . . . . Everything

     ● . . . . Clicks + Drags

TO SELECT A RECORDING AREA:

NOTE: This setting cannot be changed after the macro has been recorded.

   a) Click on . . . . Relative to: ⬇

   b) Click on . . . . Window

     OR

     Click on . . . . Screen

TO WRITE A DESCRIPTION FOR THE MACRO:

   a) Click in . . . . Description [＿＿＿]

   b) Type the macro description.

7. Click on . . . . [**Start**]

   Recorder becomes a flashing icon.

8. Type or perform actions and commands to be recorded.

9. Press . . . . [Ctrl] + [Break]
   to stop recording.

Continued ...

118

RECORDING A MACRO (continued)

10. Click on . . . . ○ S̲ave Macro
    to select (◉).

11. Click on . . . . [OK]

*Recorder remains as an icon on the desktop, and the previous
application in which macro was recorded becomes active.*

*NOTE: To reuse a macro in another Windows session, you must
open the Recorder icon and save the macro(s) to a file.
See Saving and Naming Data Files, page 25.*

SAVE CHANGES MADE TO CURRENT RECORDER FILE

See Saving and Naming Data Files, page 25.
See Saving an Existing Data File, page 25.

COMBINING MACROS SAVED IN SEPARATE RECORDER FILES

FROM RECORDER WINDOW

1. Open (page 24) or create first recorder file.

2. Click on . . . . **File**

3. Click on . . . . **Merge...**

4. Double-click in File N̲ame list box on filename
   containing macros to combine with first file.

*NOTE: Recorder removes assigned shortcut keys from incoming
file when duplications exist.*

5. Save the recorder file (pages 25 and 26).

PLAYING BACK A MACRO

TO START RECORDER AND OPEN MACRO FILE:

NOTE: *To play back a macro, Recorder must be running and a macro file, containing actions to play back, must be open.*

FROM PROGRAM MANAGER
ACCESSORIES GROUP WINDOW

a) Double-click on . . . .

Recorder

FROM RECORDER WINDOW

b) Click on . . . . **File**

c) Click on . . . . **Open...**

d) Double-click in File Name list box on name of file containing macros to play back.
See Locating Files, page 10.

TO PLAY BACK MACRO(S) FROM AN APPLICATION:

1. Run or select application in which macro(s) will be used.

FROM APPLICATION WINDOW

2. As needed, press defined shortcut key(s) to perform recorded actions.

TO PLAY BACK MACRO(S) FROM RECORDER WINDOW:

1. Click on name of macro to run.

2. Click on . . . . **Macro**

3. Click on . . . . **Run**

120

DELETING A RECORDED MACRO

FROM RECORDER WINDOW

1. Click on name of macro to delete.

2. Click on . . . . **Macro**

3. Click on . . . . **Delete**

4. Click on . . . . `OK`

CHANGING PROPERTIES OF A RECORDED MACRO

FROM RECORDER WINDOW

1. Click on name of macro to change.

2. Click on . . . . **Macro**

3. Click on . . . . **Properties...**

4. Make changes to macro properties as desired.

   NOTE: The actions of a recording and the recording area cannot be changed. See Recording a Macro, page 115, steps 4-6.

5. Click on . . . . `OK`

TURNING OFF OR ON A MACRO'S CONTROL + BREAK CHECKING

NOTE: *By default, the option below is selected (✓). Deselect the option to disable use of the Control + Break key combination while a macro is running.*

FROM RECORDER WINDOW:

1. Click on . . . . **O**ptions
2. Click on . . . . **C**ontrol+Break Checking to select (✓) or deselect.

DISABLE OR ENABLE USE OF A MACRO'S SHORTCUT KEYS

NOTE: *By default, the option below is selected (✓). Deselect the option when your current application uses the same key that has been assigned to a macro.*

FROM RECORDER WINDOW:

1. Click on . . . . **O**ptions
2. Click on . . . . **S**hortcut Keys to select (✓) or deselect.

MINIMIZING OR RETAINING RECORDER'S WINDOW DURING A MACRO PLAYBACK

NOTE: By default, the option below is selected (✓). Deselect the option to retain the Recorder window when the Run command is used to play back a macro.

FROM RECORDER WINDOW:

1. Click on . . . . **Options**

2. Click on . . . . **Minimize On Use** to select (✓) or deselect.

SETTING RECORDER DEFAULT PREFERENCES

FROM RECORDER WINDOW:

1. Click on . . . . **Options**

2. Click on . . . . **Preferences...**

3. Click on . . . . ⬇ of setting to change.

4. Click on desired setting.

5. Repeat steps 3 and 4 for each setting to change.

6. Click on . . . . **OK**

CLOSING RECORDER

See Closing an Application Window or Icon, page 23.

USING SETUP FROM WINDOWS

Use Setup from Windows to:
- *Add or change device drivers for mouse, keyboard, display and network,*

NOTE: To install print drivers see Setting Up Printers, page 110.
To install multi-media drivers, see Installing and Configuring Special Device Drivers, page 145.

- *Add applications that have been installed on the computer's hard disk to the Windows environment,*
- *Add or remove optional Window files.*

NOTE: Also see Using Setup from MS-DOS Prompt, page 126.

FROM PROGRAM MANAGER MAIN GROUP WINDOW

1. Quit all running applications if you are making changes that will require Windows to be restarted.

2. Double-click on . . . .
    Setup displays a window showing current settings.

TO CHANGE SYSTEM SETTINGS:

FROM WINDOWS SETUP WINDOW

   a) Click on . . . . **Options**

   b) Click on . . . . **Change System Settings...**

   c) Click on one of the following for item to change:

   • . . . . Display: ⬇
   • . . . . Keyboard: ⬇
   • . . . . Mouse: ⬇
   • . . . . Network: ⬇

   d) Click on name of desired item in list box.

   e) Repeat steps c and d for each item to change.

Continued ...

USING SETUP FROM WINDOWS (continued)

   f) Click on . . . .   `OK`

   IF Setup finds an existing driver,

      • Click on . . . .   `Current`

        to reinstall driver present on hard disk.

      OR

      • Click on . . . .   `New`

        to reinstall driver from its source diskette.

   g) Click on . . . .   `Restart Windows`

      OR

      Click on . . . .   `Reboot`

TO ADD APPLICATIONS INSTALLED ON HARD DISK
TO PROGRAM MANAGER GROUP WINDOWS:

   a) Click on . . . .   **Options**

   b) Click on . . . .   **Setup Applications**

   c) Click on . . . .   `OK`

   d) Click on one or more of the locations in the Setup will Search list box.

   e) Click on . . . .   `Search Now`

      IF Setup asks for a name for a found application,

        1) Click on name in list.

        2) Click on . . . .   `OK`

      Setup displays applications found in Applications_found on hard disk(s) list box.

Continued ...

USING SETUP FROM WINDOWS (continued)

f) • Click on names of applications to add in Applications found on hard disk(s) list box.

TO CANCEL A SELECTED APPLICATION:

• Click on its name a second time.

• Click on . . . . `Add ->`

OR

f) Click on . . . . `Add All`

Setup displays applications in Set up for use with Windows list box.

TO REMOVE AN APPLICATION FROM SET UP FOR USE WITH WINDOWS LIST:

• Click on its name.

• Click on . . . . `<- Remove`

g) Click on . . . . `OK`

TO ADD OR REMOVE OPTIONAL WINDOWS FILES:

FROM WINDOWS SETUP WINDOW

a) Click on . . . . **Options**

b) Click on . . **Add/Remove Windows Components**

c) Make selections as desired.

See Selecting Options in a Dialog Box, page 8.

NOTE: When files or components are added, Setup will request the Windows installation disks.

d) Click on . . . . `OK`

USING SETUP FROM MS-DOS PROMPT

Use Setup from the MS-DOS prompt to:
- *Add or change device drivers that are not supplied with Windows,*
- *Change or update device drivers,*
- *Install or reinstall Windows on a hard disk.*

NOTE: <u>*CAUTION:*</u> *Exit Windows before starting Setup from the DOS prompt.*

FROM DOS PROMPT

TO CHANGE DEVICE SETTING OR UPDATE DRIVERS:

1. • Type . . . . **CD**

   • Type name of directory containing Windows.

   EXAMPLE: CD\WINDOWS.

2. Press . . . . ⏎

OR

TO INSTALL OR REINSTALL WINDOWS:

1. • Insert Windows Disk 1 in drive A or B and close drive door.

   • Type . . . . **A:** or **B:**

2. Press . . . . ⏎

START SETUP PROGRAM:

3. Type . . . . **SETUP**

4. Press . . . . ⏎

OPENING THE CONTROL PANEL
— To Set System Defaults

FROM PROGRAM MANAGER MAIN GROUP WINDOW

• Double-click on . . . .

Control Panel

NOTE: *Changes can be made to the following settings:*
386 Enhanced (p. 147), Color (p. 127), Com. Ports (p. 132),
Date and Time (p. 142), Desktop (p. 135), Fonts (p. 130),
International (p. 140), Keyboard (p. 140), MIDI (p. 144),
Mouse (p. 134), Network (p. 144), Printers (p. 110),
Sounds (p. 143), Special Drivers (p. 145).

CHANGING SCREEN COLORS

NOTE: *Choosing solid colors may speed up screen displays and*
increase readability of text.

FROM CONTROL PANEL WINDOW

1. Double-click on . . . .

Color

Windows displays a sample screen showing
current color selections.

TO SELECT A PRESET COLOR SCHEME:

a) Click on . . . . Color Schemes: ⬇

b) Click on a color scheme name.

TO CHANGE CURRENT COLOR SCHEME:

a) Click on . . . . [Color Palette >>]

b) Click in the desktop sample on any screen
element to be changed.

OR

• Click on . . . . Screen Element: ⬇

Continued ...

CHANGING SCREEN COLORS (continued)

- Click on screen element to be changed.

c) Click on a color from <u>B</u>asic Colors or <u>C</u>ustom Colors palette.

   Also see To Define a Custom Color, below.

d) Repeat steps b and c for each screen element to be changed.

TO DEFINE AND ADD NEW COLORS TO THE CUSTOM COLORS PALETTE:

a) Click on . . . . [Define Custom Colors...]

b) Click on the box in the <u>C</u>ustom Colors Palette to receive new color.

c) Click on the up or down increment arrow of any of the following to increase or decrease color components.

- . . . . H<u>u</u>e: [⬍]

  (Selects a color on the color spectrum.)

- . . . . <u>S</u>at: [⬍]

  (Changes purity (% of gray) of color.)

- . . . . <u>L</u>um: [⬍]

  (Change brightness (black/white) of color.)

- . . . . <u>R</u>ed: [⬍]

- . . . . <u>G</u>reen: [⬍]

- . . . . <u>B</u>lue: [⬍]

OR

- Click on desired area in the color refiner box to specify a color from the full range.

Continued ...

CHANGING SCREEN COLORS (continued)

- Click, hold and drag vertical
  luminosity bar's . . . . ◁
  to increase or decrease brightness.

TO CHANGE MIXED COLOR PATTERN TO A SOLID:

- Double-click on
  right side of . . . . Color/So̲lid ⬜

d) Click on . . . . [Add Color]

Mixed color is placed in selected C̲ustom Colors palette box.

e) Repeat steps b-d for each color to be added.

f) Click on . . . . [C̲lose]

TO SAVE A COLOR SCHEME:

a) Click on . . . . [Sa̲ve Scheme]

b) Type a name for color scheme.

c) Click on . . . . [OK]

TO REMOVE A SAVED COLOR SCHEME:

a) Click on . . . . Color S̲chemes: ⬇

b) Click on name of color scheme to be removed.

c) Click on . . . . [Rem̲ove Scheme]

d) Click on . . . . [Y̲es]

2. Click on . . . . [OK]

130

CHANGING SCREEN AND PRINTER FONTS

NOTE: The steps below provide a way to add or remove screen/printer fonts.   These fonts can be used with any Windows application.

FROM CONTROL PANEL WINDOW

1.   Double-click on . . . .   **Fonts**

TO ADD SCREEN/PRINTER FONTS:

   a) Click on . . . .   `Add...`

   b) If necessary, change current drive or directory.
      See Locating Files, page 10.

   c) Press . . . .   `Ctrl`
      <u>and</u> click on each font to be added in
      List of <u>F</u>onts list box.

      OR

      Click on . . . .   `Select All`

   d) Click on . . . .   `OK`

TO REMOVE FONTS:

NOTE: <u>CAUTION</u>: Do not remove the MS Sans Serif font. Windows uses this font to display dialog box information.

   a) Press . . . .   `Ctrl`
      <u>and</u> click on each font to be removed in
      Installed <u>F</u>onts list box.

   b) Click on . . . .   `Remove`

TO DELETE FONT FILE FROM DISK:

   • Click on . . . . ☐ <u>D</u>elete Font File From Disk
      to select (☒).

Continued ...

CHANGING SCREEN AND PRINTER FONTS (continued)

c) Click on . . . . [<u>Y</u>es]

to remove one font at a time.

OR

Click on . . . . [Yes To <u>A</u>ll]

to remove all selected fonts.

TO SET SPECIAL TRUETYPE OPTIONS:

*NOTE: Changes made will not take effect until Windows
         is restarted.*

• Click on . . . . [True Type...]

TO DISABLE USE OF TRUETYPE FONTS:

• Click on . . . . ☒ Enable TrueType Fonts
to deselect (☐).

TO USE TRUETYPE FONTS EXCLUSIVELY:

1) Click on

☐ <u>S</u>how Only TrueType Fonts in Application
to select (☒).

2) Click on . . . . [OK]

2. Click on . . . . [Close]

CONFIGURING A COMMUNICATION PORT

FROM CONTROL PANEL WINDOW

1. Double-click on . . . .

    Ports

TO CHANGE SETTINGS FOR A COM (SERIAL) PORT:

   a) Click on Com icon to be changed.

   b) Click on . . . . `Settings...`

   TO CHANGE BAUD RATE:

   1) Click on . . . . Baud Rate: ⬇

   2) Click on a baud rate.

   TO CHANGE DATA BITS SETTING:

   1) Click on . . . . Data Bits: ⬇

   2) Click on a data bits setting.

   TO CHANGE THE PARITY SETTING:

   1) Click on . . . . Parity: ⬇

   2) Click on a parity setting.

   TO CHANGE THE STOP BITS SETTING:

   1) Click on . . . . Stop Bits: ⬇

   2) Click on a stop bits setting.

   TO CHANGE THE FLOW CONTROL SETTING:

   1) Click on . . . . Flow Control: ⬇

   2) Click on a flow control setting.

Continued ...

CONFIGURING A COMMUNICATION PORT (continued)

TO CHANGE ADVANCED SETTING (Base I/O & IRQ):

1) Click on . . . . `Advanced...`

TO CHANGE BASE I/O ADDRESS:

a. Click on . . . . Base I/O Port Address: `⬇`

b. Click on an address value.

TO CHANGE THE IRQ SETTING:

a. Click on Interrupt Request Line (IRQ): `⬇`

b. Click on an IRQ number.

2) Click on . . . . `OK`

to accept advanced setting(s).

c) Click on . . . . `OK`

to accept port settings.

2. Click on . . . . `Close`

CUSTOMIZING MOUSE

FROM CONTROL PANEL WINDOW

1. Double-click on . . . .

Mouse

TO CHANGE TRACKING SPEED:

-   Click on left or right Mouse Tracking Speed scroll arrow until desired speed is set.

TO CHANGE DOUBLE-CLICK SPEED:

-   Click on left or right Double-Click Speed scroll arrow until desired speed is set.

TO CHANGE PRIMARY MOUSE BUTTON:

NOTE: *By default, the left mouse button is the primary button.*

-   Click on . . . . ☐ Swap Left/Right Buttons to select (☒).

TO SET MOUSE TO LEAVE A TRAIL:

NOTE: *This setting is useful for LCD displays.*

-   Click on . . . . ☐ Mouse Trails to select (☒).

2. Click on . . . . OK

CUSTOMIZING THE DESKTOP

FROM CONTROL PANEL WINDOW

1. Double-click on . . . .

Desktop

TO USE FAST APPLICATION SWITCHING:

*   Click on . . . . ☐ Fast "Alt+Tab" Switching
    to select (☒).

    NOTE: When this option is selected, the name of the next application you will switch to is displayed each time you press Tab while pressing and holding the Alt key.

TO CHANGE TO A PRESET DESKTOP PATTERN:

a) Click on . . . . Pattern Name: ⬇

b) Click on a pattern name.

TO CREATE A DESKTOP PATTERN:

a) Click on . . . . [Edit Pattern...]

b) Type new pattern name in . . . Name: [   ]

c) Click on pattern display area to
    add/subtract elements.

d) Click on . . . . [Add]

e) Click on . . . . [OK]

TO EDIT A DESKTOP PATTERN:

a) Click on . . . . [Edit Pattern...]

b) Click on . . . . Name: ⬇

c) Click on a pattern name.

Continued ...

136

CUSTOMIZING THE DESKTOP (continued)

    d) Click on pattern display area to add/subtract elements.

    e) Click on . . . . | Change |

    f) Click on . . . . | OK |

TO REMOVE A DESKTOP PATTERN:

    a) Click on . . . . | Edit Pattern... |

    b) Click on . . . . Name: ⬇

    c) Click on pattern name to be removed.

    d) Click on . . . . | Remove |

    e) Click on . . . . | Yes |

    f) Click on . . . . | OK |

TO SELECT A WALLPAPER PATTERN:

NOTE: Choosing a wallpaper will use additional memory.

    a) Click on . . . . Wallpaper File: ⬇

    b) Click on a wallpaper pattern name.

TO ARRANGE A WALLPAPER PATTERN:

    • Click on . . . . ○ Center
      (centers wallpaper on desktop).

      OR

      Click on . . . . ○ Tile
      (covers desktop with wallpaper).

      Selected option contains a dark circle (◉).

Continued ...

CUSTOMIZING THE DESKTOP (continued)

TO CHANGE CURSOR BLINK RATE:

- Click on left or right Cursor Blink Rate scroll arrow until desired speed is set.

TO CHANGE SPACING BETWEEN ICONS:

- Click on up or down . . . . . Icons Spacing: [▲▼] until desired number appears.

TO WRAP ICON TITLES:

- Click on . . . . [ ] Wrap Titles to select (⊠).

TO SET SPACING OF DESKTOP ELEMENTS TO INVISIBLE GRID:

- Click on up or down . . . . Granularity: [▲▼]

    NOTE: The larger the number, the greater the distance between desktop elements.

TO CHANGE WINDOW BORDER WIDTH:

- Click on up or down . . . . . Border Width: [▲▼] until desired number appears.

TO SELECT A SCREEN SAVER DISPLAY:

a) Click on . . . . Screen Saver Name: [↓]

b) Click on a screen saver name.

TO SET SCREEN SAVER DELAY TIME:

- Click on up or down . . . . Delay: [▲▼] until desired number appears.

Continued ...

138

CUSTOMIZING THE DESKTOP (continued)

TO TEST APPEARANCE OF SELECTED SCREEN SAVER:

- Click on . . . . [Te̲st]

TO SET SCREEN SAVER PASSWORD OPTIONS:

NOTE: *The password, but not the password status (on/off), is carried over when you select a different screen saver name.*

a) Click on . . . . [Set̲up...]

b) Click on . . . . □ Password Protected
   to select (⊠) or deselect (□).

c) Click on . . . . [S̲et Password...]

> #### TO REMOVE OR CHANGE AN EXISTING PASSWORD:
>
> - Type old password
>   in . . . . O̲ld Password: [   ]
>
> #### TO SPECIFY A NEW PASSWORD:
>
> 1) Click in . . . . . . N̲ew Password: [   ]
>
> 2) Type a password.
>
> > *NOTE:* *C̲A̲U̲T̲I̲O̲N̲: If you forget your password, you will have to reboot in order to use Windows, and it will not be possible to save data in any open documents.*
>
> 3) Click in . . R̲etype New Password: [   ]
>
> 4) Type identical password.
>
> 5) Click on . . . . [OK]

d) Click on . . . . [OK]

Continued ...

CUSTOMIZING THE DESKTOP (continued)

TO SET OTHER SCREEN SAVER OPTIONS:

a) Click on . . . . [Setup...]

>   NOTE: Available options depend upon the selected Screen
>   Saver name.

b) Select options as desired.
See Selecting Options in a Dialog Box, page 8.

c) Click on . . . . [OK]

2. Click on . . . . [OK]

CONTROLLING PRINTERS

*See Setting Up Printers — From Print Manager or Control Panel,
page 110.*

140

CHANGING KEYBOARD TYPING SPEED

FROM CONTROL PANEL WINDOW

1. Double-click on . . . . ▦ Keyboard

TO CHANGE DELAY BEFORE FIRST REPEAT:

- Click on left or right <u>D</u>elay Before First Repeat scroll arrow until desired speed is set.

TO CHANGE KEY REPEAT RATE:

- Click on left or right <u>R</u>epeat Rate scroll arrow until desired speed is set.

TO TEST KEYBOARD REPEAT RATE:

a) Click in . . . . <u>T</u>est: [＿＿＿]

b) Press and hold any character.

2. Click on . . . . [OK]

CHANGING INTERNATIONAL SETTINGS

FROM CONTROL PANEL WINDOW

1. Double-click on . . . . 🌐 International

TO CHANGE COUNTRY SETTING:

a) Click on . . . . <u>C</u>ountry: 🔽

b) Click on desired country.

TO CHANGE LANGUAGE SETTING:

a) Click on . . . . <u>L</u>anguage: 🔽

b) Click on desired language format.

Continued ...

CHANGING INTERNATIONAL SETTINGS (continued)

TO CHANGE KEYBOARD LAYOUT:

    a) Click on . . . . Keyboard Layout: ⬇

    b) Click on desired keyboard layout.

TO CHANGE MEASUREMENT SYSTEM:

    a) Click on . . . . Measurement: ⬇

    b) Click on desired measurement system.

TO CHANGE LIST SEPARATOR CHARACTER:

    a) Double-click in . . . . List Separator: ☐

    b) Type new list separator character.

TO CHANGE DATE, CURRENCY, TIME OR NUMBER FORMATS:

    a) Click on . . . . [Change...]

       in group box of format to be altered.

    b) Select options as desired.
       See Selecting Options in a Dialog Box, page 8.

    c) Click on . . . . [OK]

2. Click on . . . . [OK]

142

CHANGING SYSTEM DATE AND TIME

FROM CONTROL PANEL WINDOW

1. Double-click on . . . . Date/Time

TO CHANGE DATE:

   a) Double-click on number to change in Date box.

   b) Type a new number.

   c) Repeat steps a and b for each number to be changed.

TO CHANGE TIME:

   a) Double-click on number to change in Time box.

   b) Type a new number.

   c) Repeat steps a and b for each number to be changed.

TO SPECIFY AM OR PM:

   a) Click on time suffix.

   b) Press **A** (AM)

   OR

   Press **P** (PM).

2. Click on . . . . OK

ASSIGNING SOUNDS TO EVENTS

FROM CONTROL PANEL WINDOW

1. Double-click on . . . .

    Sound

TO ASSIGN SOUNDS TO AN EVENT:

NOTE: Requires installation of a sound card and driver.

   a) Click on event to receive a sound in Events
      list box.

   b) Click on a sound file in Files list box.

      NOTE: To remove a sound from an event, click on <none>.

   c) Repeat steps a and b for each event to receive a
      sound.

TO TEST SOUND:

NOTE: Requires installation of a sound card and driver.

   • Click on . . . .   Test

TO SET WARNING BEEP/SOUNDS ON OR OFF:

   • Click on . . . . ☒ Enable System Sounds
      to select (☒) or deselect (☐).

2. Click on . . . .   OK

144

SELECTING A MIDI SETUP FOR AN INSTALLED SOUND DEVICE

FROM CONTROL PANEL WINDOW

1. Double-click on . . . .

   MIDI Mapper

2. Click on . . . . Name: ⬇

3. Click on a setup name.

4. Click on . . . . Close

NOTE: Windows also provides commands to create or edit setups, patch maps, and key maps. Refer to your Windows sound device documentation.

CHANGING NETWORK SETTINGS

FROM CONTROL PANEL WINDOW

1. Double-click on . . . .

   Network

NOTE: Options available depend upon type of network connection.

Possible options include:

• Beginning and ending a network session. (Logging on and off.)

• Sending messages to other network users.

• Changing user ID and password.

• Restoring network connections when Windows is restarted.

2. Click on . . . . OK

INSTALLING AND CONFIGURING SPECIAL DEVICE DRIVERS

FROM CONTROL PANEL WINDOW

1. Double-click on . . . .

Drivers

TO INSTALL A NEW DEVICE DRIVER:

a) Click on . . . . [**A̲dd...**]

b) Click on driver to add in L̲ist of Drivers list box.

c) Click on . . . . [OK]

d) If necessary, type path to indicate location of driver files.

e) If necessary, insert disk in specified drive.

f) Click on . . . . [OK]

g) IF installed driver requires additional settings, select from available options in Setup dialog box.

> NOTE: <u>CAUTION</u>: Settings must not conflict with existing devices. Refer to manual for your device for information about its settings.

h) Click on . . . . [OK]

> NOTE: Depending upon device installed, additional settings may be required. You may have to restart Windows in order to use a new device driver.

TO CHANGE SETTING FOR A DEVICE DRIVER:

a) Click on device driver to change in I̲nstalled Drivers list box.

Continued ...

146

INSTALLING AND CONFIGURING SPECIAL DEVICE DRIVERS (continued)

b) Click on . . . . [**Setup...**]

c) Select from available options.

NOTE: Refer to manual for your device.

d) Click on . . . . [**OK**]

NOTE: You may have to restart Windows in order to have changes take effect.

TO REMOVE A DEVICE DRIVER:

a) Click on device driver to remove in Installed Drivers list box.

b) Click on . . . . [**Remove**]

c) Click on . . . . [**Yes**]

NOTE: You may have to restart Windows in order to have changes take effect.

2. Click on . . . . [**Close**]

CHANGING 386 ENHANCED MODE SETTINGS

FROM CONTROL PANEL WINDOW

1. Double-click on . . . .

386 Enhanced

TO CONTROL SIMULTANEOUS USE OF PORTS:

a) Click on port connected to device to be controlled in <u>D</u>evice Contention list box.

b) Click on one of the following:

● . . . . ○ <u>A</u>lways Warn

● . . . . ○ <u>N</u>ever Warn

● . . . . ○ Idle (in sec.)

Selected option contains a dark circle (◉).

IF Idle (in sec.) is selected,

● Click on up or down . . Idle (in sec.) to set a time.

TO CHANGE APPLICATIONS SCHEDULING DURING MULTITASKING:

NOTE: *A time slice is the amount of processor time given to an application before the next application receives control. A time slice is measured in milliseconds.*

TO SPECIFY TIME SLICE FOR THE ACTIVE WINDOWS PROGRAM:

● Click on up or down . . . . . . Windows in <u>F</u>oreground until desired number (1-10,000) appears.

Continued ...

CHANGING 386 ENHANCED MODE SETTINGS
(continued)

TO SPECIFY TIME SLICE FOR WINDOWS APPLICATIONS WHEN A NON-WINDOWS PROGRAM IS ACTIVE:

- Click on up

  or down . . . . . . Windows in Background ⬜⬆⬇

  until desired number (1-10,000) appears.

TO SET EXCLUSIVE USE OF PROCESSING TIME FOR WINDOWS APPLICATIONS:

- Click on . . . . ⬜ Exclusive in Foreground
  to select (⊠).

  *NOTE: When this is selected, Windows applications will
  receive all of the processing time, while non-
  Windows applications in the background
  receive none.*

TO SPECIFY HOW APPLICATIONS SHARE PROCESSING TIME:

- Click on up

  or down . . Minimum Timeslice (in msec) ⬜⬆⬇

  until desired number (1-10,000) appears.

  *NOTE: Number represents minimum processor time (in
  milliseconds) devoted to application before Windows
  will give processor control to another application.*

TO CHANGE SWAP FILE SETTINGS FOR VIRTUAL MEMORY:

a) Click on . . . . [**Virtual Memory...**]

b) Click on . . . . [**Change >>**]

TO SET LOCATION OF SWAP FILE:

1) Click on . . . . Drive: ⬇

2) Click on desired drive label.

Continued ...

CHANGING 386 ENHANCED MODE SETTINGS
(continued)

TO SPECIFY TYPE OF SWAP FILE TO USE:

1) Click on . . . . Type: ⬇

2) Click on one of the following:

- ● . . . . Temporary

- ● . . . . Permanent

- ● . . . . None

TO SPECIFY SIZE OF SWAP FILE:

1) Double-click in . . . . . . New Size: [   ]

2) Type a number.

> *NOTE: Number represents size in kilobytes of swap file.*

c) Click on . . . . [OK]

TO SET SYSTEM FOR 32-BIT DISK ACCESS:

- Click on . . . . ☐ Use 32-Bit Disk Access to select (☒).

2. Click on . . . . [OK]

150

EMBEDDING AN OBJECT—STARTING FROM THE RECEIVING APPLICATION

1. Run or select application to receive object.

   NOTE: Application must support object linking and embedding (i.e., Write or Cardfile).

2. Open or create file to receive object.

3. If applicable, place insertion point where object will be placed.

IF   Cardfile is the receiving application,

- Click on . . . . **Edit**
- Click on . . . . **Pictu<u>r</u>e**

4. Click on . . . . **Edit**

5. Click on . . . . **<u>I</u>nsert Object...**

6. Double-click on a source application in <u>O</u>bject Type list box.

FROM SOURCE APPLICATION

7.   • Create file to be embedded.

   OR

   - Click on . . . . **Edit**
   - Click on . . . . **Paste <u>F</u>rom...**

     OR

   - Click on . . . . **<u>I</u>nsert File...**
   - Double-click on filename of document to be embedded.

8. Click on . . . . **<u>F</u>ile**

9. Click on . . . . **<u>U</u>pdate**

Continued ...

EMBEDDING AN OBJECT — STARTING FROM THE RECEIVING APPLICATION (continued)

10. Click on . . . . **File**
11. Click on . . . . **E<u>x</u>it**

EMBEDDING AN OBJECT–STARTING FROM THE SOURCE APPLICATION

1. Run or select application from which object will be created.

   NOTE: Application must support object linking and embedding (i.e., Paintbrush or Sound Recorder).

2. Open or create a file containing object to be embedded.

3. If applicable, select part of document to embed.

4. Click on . . . . **<u>E</u>dit**
5. Click on . . . . **<u>C</u>opy**

6. Run or select application to receive object.

   NOTE: Application must support object linking and embedding (i.e., Write or Cardfile).

FROM RECEIVING APPLICATION

7. Open or create file to receive object.

8. If applicable, place insertion point where object will be placed.

Continued ...

EMBEDDING AN OBJECT — STARTING FROM THE SOURCE APPLICATION (continued)

IF   Cardfile is the receiving application,

- Click on . . . . **Edit**
- Click on . . . . **Picture**

9. Click on . . . . **Edit**

10. Click on . . . . **Paste**

    OR

    TO SPECIFY FORMAT PRIOR TO PASTING THE OBJECT:

    a) Click on . . . . **Paste Special...**

    b) Click on format to use in **D**ata Type list box.

    c) Click on . . . . `Paste`

NOTE: *If a sound file has been embedded, a Sound Recorder icon appears. To play back the sound, double-click on the icon.*

EDITING AN EMBEDDED OBJECT

FROM APPLICATION CONTAINING EMBEDDED OBJECT

IF   Cardfile is the current application,

- Click on . . . . **Edit**
- Click on . . . . **Picture**

IF   editing a sound object,

1. • Click on sound icon.
   - Click on . . . . **Edit**
   - Click on . . . . **Sound Object** ▸
   - Click on . . . . **Edit**

OR

IF   editing any other object type,

1. Double-click on embedded object.
   Source application and document appear.

FROM SOURCE DOCUMENT

2. Make changes as desired.
3. Click on . . . . **File**
4. Click on . . . . **Update**
5. Click on . . . . **File**
6. Click on . . . . **Exit**

LINKING AN OBJECT TO A DOCUMENT

1. Run or select application from which object originates.

   NOTE: Application must support object linking and embedding (i.e., Paintbrush or Sound Recorder).

2. Create or open file to be linked.

3. Save the file.

4. If applicable, select part of file to be linked.

5. Click on . . . . **Edit**

6. Click on . . . . **Copy**

7. Run or select application to receive object.

   NOTE: Application must support object linking and embedding (i.e., Write or Cardfile).

FROM RECEIVING APPLICATION

8. Open or create file to receive object.

9. If applicable, place insertion point where object will be placed.

IF Cardfile is the receiving application,

   • Click on . . . . **Edit**

   • Click on . . . . **Picture**

10. Click on . . . . **Edit**

11. Click on . . . . **Paste Link**

    OR

Continued ...

LINKING AN OBJECT TO A DOCUMENT (continued)

TO SPECIFY FORMAT PRIOR TO PASTING THE LINK:

a) Click on . . . . **Paste Special...**

b) Click on format to use in Data Type list box.

c) Click on . . . . | Paste Link |

NOTE: *If a sound file has been linked, a Sound Recorder icon*
appears. To play back the sound, double-click on the icon.

EDITING A LINKED OBJECT

NOTE: *Changes made to a linked object affect all linked objects*
associated with the source document.

FROM APPLICATION CONTAINING LINKED OBJECT

IF   Cardfile is the current application,

- Click on . . . . **Edit**

- Click on . . . . **Picture**

IF   editing a sound object,

1. • Click on sound icon.

- Click on . . . . **Edit**

- Click on . . . . **Sound Object** ▸

- Click on . . . . **Edit**

OR

IF   editing any other linked object type,

1. Double-click on embedded object.
   Source application and document appear.

Continued ...

156

EDITING A LINKED OBJECT (continued)

FROM SOURCE DOCUMENT

2. Make changes as desired.

   NOTE: Linked object in receiving document is updated as changes are made.

3. Save the file.

4. Click on . . . . **File**

5. Click on . . . . **Exit**

CHANGING HOW LINKED OBJECTS ARE UPDATED

FROM APPLICATION CONTAINING LINKED OBJECT

IF Cardfile is the current application,

- Click on . . . . **Edit**

- Click on . . . . **Picture**

1. Click on . . . . **Edit**

2. Click on . . . . **Links...**

3. Click on link to change in Links list box.

4. Click on . . . . ○ Automatic

   OR

   Click on . . . . ○ Manual
   to select (◉).

5. Click on . . . . [OK]

UPDATING A MANUALLY LINKED OBJECT

FROM APPLICATION CONTAINING LINKED OBJECT

IF   Cardfile is the current application,

- Click on . . . . **Edit**
- Click on . . . . **Pictur̲e**

1. Click on . . . . **Edit**
2. Click on . . . . **Lin̲ks...**
3. Click on link to update in L̲inks list box.
4. Click on . . . . **[Update Now]**
5. Click on . . . . **[OK]**

158

COPYING AN EXISTING LINK

FROM APPLICATION CONTAINING LINKED OBJECT

IF   Cardfile is the current application,

- Click on . . . . **Edit**
- Click on . . . . **Picture**

1.   Click on object.

2.   Click on . . . . **Edit**

3.   Click on . . . . **Copy**

4.   Run or select application to receive object.

   *NOTE: Application must support object linking and embedding
        (i.e., Write or Cardfile).*

FROM RECEIVING APPLICATION

5.   Open or create file to receive object.

6.   If applicable, place insertion point where object
     will be placed.

IF   Cardfile is the receiving application,

- Click on . . . . **Edit**
- Click on . . . . **Picture**

7.   Click on . . . . **Edit**

8.   Click on . . . . **Paste**

BREAKING A LINK

FROM APPLICATION CONTAINING LINKED OBJECT

IF   Cardfile is the current application,

- Click on . . . . **Edit**
- Click on . . . . **Pictur**e

1. Click on object.

2. Click on . . . . **Edit**

3. Click on . . . . **Links...**

4. Click on . . . . [Cancel Link]

5. Click on . . . . [OK]

FIXING OR CHANGING A LINK

FROM APPLICATION CONTAINING LINKED OBJECT

IF   Cardfile is the current application,

- Click on . . . . **Edit**
- Click on . . . . **Pictur**e

1. Click on object.

2. Click on . . . . **Edit**

3. Click on . . . . **Links...**

4. Click on . . . . [Change Link...]

5. Double-click on source filename in File **N**ame
   list box.
   See Locating Files, page 10.

6. Click on . . . . [OK]

DELETING A LINK

FROM APPLICATION CONTAINING LINKED OBJECT

IF   Cardfile is the current application,

- Click on . . . . **Edit**
- Click on . . . . **Pictur<u>e</u>**

1.   Click on object.

2.   Click on . . . . **<u>E</u>dit**

3.   Click on . . . . **Cu<u>t</u>**

USING OBJECT PACKAGER TO PACKAGE AN ENTIRE DOCUMENT

1.   Run Object Packager (page 12).

2.   Click on . . . . **<u>F</u>ile**

3.   Click on . . . . **<u>I</u>mport...**

4.   Double-click on filename to be packaged in File <u>N</u>ame list box.

    See Locating Files, page 10.

    Application icon appears in Appearance window, and Filename appears in Content window.

5.   Click on . . . . **<u>E</u>dit**

6.   Click on . . . . **Copy Pac<u>k</u>age**

7.   Run or select application to receive the package.

    NOTE: Application must support object linking and embedding (i.e., Write or Cardfile).

Continued ...

USING OBJECT PACKAGER TO PACKAGE AN ENTIRE DOCUMENT — (continued)

FROM RECEIVING APPLICATION

8. Open or create file to receive object.

9. If applicable, place insertion point where object will be placed.

IF Cardfile is the receiving application,

- Click on . . . . **Edit**

- Click on . . . . **Picture**

10. Click on . . . . **Edit**

11. Click on . . . . **Paste**

Package appears as an icon in the document. Double-click on icon to view or play back its contents.

USING OBJECT PACKAGER TO PACKAGE PART OF A DOCUMENT

1. Run or select the application from which object originates.

    NOTE: Application must support object linking and embedding (i.e., Paintbrush).

2. Create or open file containing object to be packaged.

IF linking the object,

- Save the file.

3. Select part of file to be packaged.

4. Click on . . . . **Edit**

Continued ...

USING OBJECT PACKAGER TO PACKAGE PART OF A DOCUMENT (continued)

5. Click on . . . . **Copy**

6. Run or select Object Packager.

FROM OBJECT PACKAGER

7. Click on . . . . **Edit**

TO EMBED THE OBJECT:

• Click on . . . . **Paste**

OR

TO LINK THE OBJECT:

• Click on . . . . **Paste Link**

8. Click on . . . . **Edit**

9. Click on . . . . **Copy Package**

10. Run or select application to receive object.

> *NOTE: Application must support object linking and embedding (i.e., Write or Cardfile).*

FROM RECEIVING APPLICATION

11. Open or create file to receive object.

12. If applicable, place insertion point where object will be placed.

IF Cardfile is the receiving application,

• Click on . . . . **Edit**

• Click on . . . . **Picture**

13. Click on . . . . **Edit**

14. Click on . . . . **Paste**

Package appears as an icon in the document. Double-click on icon to view its contents.

PACKAGING AN MS-DOS COMMAND LINE

1. Run Object Packager (page 12).

2. Click on . . . . **Edit**

3. Click on . . . . **Command Line...**

4. Type an MS-DOS command or program filename.

   NOTE: If necessary, include path where file is located.
   EXAMPLE: c:\batch\jetstart

5. Click on . . . . | OK |

6. Click on . . . . | Insert Icon... |

7. Double-click on an icon in Current Icon list.

8. Click on . . . . **Edit**

9. Click on . . . . **Copy Package**

10. Run or select application to receive the package.

    NOTE: Application must support object linking and embedding
    (i.e., Write or Cardfile).

FROM RECEIVING APPLICATION

11. Open or create file to receive object.

12. If applicable, place insertion point where object will be placed.

IF Cardfile is the receiving application,

   • Click on . . . . **Edit**

   • Click on . . . . **Picture**

13. Click on . . . . **Edit**

14. Click on . . . . **Paste**

Package appears as an icon in the document. Double-click on icon
to execute command or run program specified in command line.

164

CHANGING A PACKAGE ICON

FROM OBJECT PACKAGER WINDOW

1. Click on . . . . `Insert Icon...`

TO CHANGE THE ICON LIST:

- Type path and name
  of source file in . . . . File Name: [＿＿＿]

  EXAMPLE: C:\WINDOWS\MORICONS.DLL

  OR

  a) Click on . . . . `Browse...`

  b) Double-click on filename containing icons in
     File Name list box.

     See Locating Files, page 10.

  *NOTE: Icons may be stored in files with EXE, ICO, or DLL
  filename extensions. MORICONS.DLL contains
  non-Windows application icons, and PROGMAN.EXE
  contains Windows application icons.*

2. Double-click on desired icon.

CHANGING A PACKAGE ICON TITLE

FROM OBJECT PACKAGER WINDOW

1. Click on . . . . **Edit**

2. Click on . . . . **Label...**

3. Type a title in . . . . Label: [＿＿＿]

4. Click on . . . . `OK`

USING FILE MANAGER AND OBJECT PACKAGER TO CREATE A PACKAGE

FROM FILE MANAGER WINDOW

FROM DIRECTORY TREE
(The left half of the directory window)

1. Click on directory name's . . . . ⬜
   containing file to be packaged.

FROM DIRECTORY CONTENTS LIST
(The right half of the directory window)

2. Click on filename to be packaged.

   > *NOTE: The file must be an application or
   > an associated data file.*

3. Click on . . . . **File**

4. Click on . . . . **Copy...**

5. Click on . . . . ○ **C̲opy to Clipboard**
   to select (◉).

6. Click on . . . . [**OK**]

7. Run Object Packager.

8. Click on . . . . **Edit**

TO PACKAGE A LINK TO A DOCUMENT:

- Click on . . . . **Paste L̲ink**

OR

TO PACKAGE AN EMBEDDED DOCUMENT:

- Click on . . . . **P̲aste**

9. Click on . . . . **Edit**

10. Click on . . . . **Copy Pac̲kage**

Continued ...

166

USING FILE MANAGER AND OBJECT PACKAGER TO CREATE A PACKAGE (continued)

11. Run or select application to receive the package.

   NOTE: Application must support object linking and embedding (i.e., Write or Cardfile).

FROM RECEIVING APPLICATION

12. Open or create file to receive object.

13. If applicable, place insertion point where object will be placed.

IF   Cardfile is the receiving application,

   • Click on . . . . **Edit**

   • Click on . . . . **Picture**

14. Click on . . . . **Edit**

15. Click on . . . . **Paste**

Package appears as an icon in the document. Double-click on icon to view or play back its contents.

USING FILE MANAGER TO CREATE A PACKAGE

FROM FILE MANAGER WINDOW

FROM DIRECTORY TREE
(The left half of the directory window)

1. Click on directory name's .... 🗀
   containing file to be packaged.

FROM DIRECTORY CONTENTS LIST
(The right half of the directory window)

2. Click on filename to be packaged.

   > *NOTE: The file must be an application or an associated data file.*

3. Click on .... **File**

4. Click on .... **Copy...**

5. Click on .... ◯ **C**opy to Clipboard
   to select (◉).

6. Click on .... [**OK**]

7. Run or select application to receive package.

   > *NOTE: Application must support object linking and embedding (i.e., Write or Cardfile).*

FROM RECEIVING APPLICATION

8. Open or create file to receive object.

9. If applicable, place insertion point where object will be placed.

Continued ...

168

USING FILE MANAGER TO CREATE A PACKAGE
(continued)

IF   Cardfile is the receiving application,

- Click on . . . . **Edit**
- Click on . . . . **Picture**

10. Click on . . . . **Edit**

TO PACKAGE A LINK TO A DOCUMENT:

- Click on . . . . **Paste Link**

OR

TO PACKAGE AN EMBEDDED DOCUMENT:

- Click on . . . . **Paste**

Package appears as an icon in the document. Double-click on icon to view or play back its contents.

USING FILE MANAGER AND A MOUSE TO CREATE A PACKAGE

NOTE: Not all applications support this procedure.

FROM FILE MANAGER WINDOW

FROM DIRECTORY TREE
(The left half of the directory window)

1.   Click on directory name's . . . . 📁

containing file to be packaged.

2.   Run or select application to receive the package.

> *NOTE: Application must support object linking and embedding (i.e., Write or Cardfile).*

Continued ...

USING FILE MANAGER AND A MOUSE TO CREATE
A PACKAGE (continued)

FROM RECEIVING APPLICATION

3. Open or create file to receive package.

4. Arrange desktop so that File Manager window and receiving application window are both in view.

FROM DIRECTORY CONTENTS LIST
(The right half of the directory window)

5. Click on source filename to be packaged.

    NOTE: The file must be an application or an associated data file.

TO PACKAGE AN EMBEDDED FILE:

a) Click, hold and drag source file onto the receiving application's document window.
    Pointer becomes a ⬚ *when placed on destination window.*

b) Release mouse button.

OR

TO PACKAGE A LINKED FILE:

a) Press . . . . **Shift** + **Ctrl**
    <u>and</u> click, hold and drag source file
    onto the receiving application's document window.
    Pointer becomes a ⬚ *when placed on destination window.*

b) Release mouse button.

170

CREATING OR EDITING A PIF FILE

NOTE: A PIF is a program information file that Windows uses to run non-Windows applications efficiently.

FROM PROGRAM MANAGER MAIN GROUP WINDOW

NOTE: The PIF Editor program item icon will be found in the Accessories group if you have upgraded from Windows 3.0.

1. Double-click on . . . .

   PIF Editor

   PIF Editor window appears, showing settings for the current operating mode.

TO OPEN AN EXISTING PIF FILE:

   a) Click on . . . . **File**

   b) Click on . . . . **Open...**

   c) Double-click on desired PIF file in File Name list box.

      See Locating Files, page 10.

TO CHANGE PIF MODE:

NOTE: Change the PIF mode to create a PIF file for an operating mode other than the current mode.

   a) Click on . . . . **Mode**

   NOTE: A check mark before the option name indicates the current operating mode.

   b) Click on . . . . **Standard**

      OR

      Click on . . . . **386 Enhanced**
      to select (✓).

2. Make entries or changes to options as desired.
   See Selecting Dialog Box Options, page 8.
   See Tables of PIF Editor Options that follow.

3. Save (page 25) the file.

Continued ...

CREATING OR EDITING A PIF FILE (continued)

Table of Standard PIF Editor Options:

Standard PIF Fields	Description
Program Filename:	Enter a pathname and application name.
Window Title:	Enter name to appear as title of program.
Optional Parameters:	Enter parameters that would be typed after program filename when starting application from MS-DOS.
Start-up Directory:	Enter a drive and pathname to be made current when application is started.
Video Mode:	Select Text or Graphics/Multiple Text to tell Windows how application uses the display.
Memory Requirements:	Specify minimal conventional memory required to start application in KB Required text box.
XMS Memory:	Specify extended memory required to start application in KB Required text box. Specify maximum amount of extended memory to allocate to the application in KB Limit text box.
Directly Modifies:	Select port (COM1-COM4) to which application will have exclusive rights. Select Keyboard if application takes direct control over keyboard.
No Screen Exchange:	Select to prevent copying information to Clipboard with Print Screen. Use to conserve memory.
Prevent Program Switch:	Select to prevent switching from this application to Windows desktop. Use to conserve memory.
Close Window on Exit:	Deselect to keep application's screen output in view when application ends.
No Save Screen	Select when the application can retain its own screen information and to tell Windows not to save in memory the application's screen information.
Reserve Shortcut Keys:	Select shortcut keys if application requires the selected key(s) for its own purposes.

172

CREATING OR EDITING A PIF FILE (continued)

Table of 386 Enhanced PIF Editor Options:

386 PIF Fields	Description
Program Filename:	Enter pathname and application name.
Window Title:	Enter name to appear as title of program.
Optional Parameters:	Enter parameters that would be typed after program filename when starting application from MS-DOS.
Start-up Directory:	Enter drive and pathname to be made current when application is started.
Video Memory:	Select Text, Low Graphics or High Graphics to tell Windows how application uses display when it's started.
Memory Requirements:	Specify conventional memory required to start application in KB Required text box. Specify maximum amount of conventional memory to allocate to the application in KB Desired text box.
EMS Memory:	Specify minimum amount of expanded memory required by application in KB Required text box. Specify maximum amount of expanded memory to allocate to the application in the KB Limit text box.
XMS Memory:	Specify minimum amount of extended memory required for your application in the KB Required text box. Specify the maximum amount of extended memory to allocate to the application in the KB Limit text box.
Display Usage:	Select Full Screen or Windowed to specify how application is displayed when started.
Execution:	Select Background to allow application to run in background while using another application in foreground. Select Exclusive to suspend other applications while this application is running in foreground.
Close Window on Exit:	Deselect to keep application's screen output in view when application ends.
Advanced...	Provides the following options: multitasking, memory, display, paste speed, ability to close application when active, reserving shortcut keys, assigning a shortcut key to activate the application.

CALCULATOR

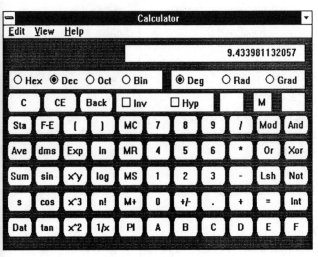

Standard Calculator

Scientific Calculator

Start Calculator by double-clicking on the Calculator program icon in the Accessories group window. (See Running an Application from a Group Window, page 12.)

With Calculator, the user may

- Perform calculations.
- Store values in memory.
- Copy and paste data to and from the Clipboard.
- Choose between Standard and Scientific calculators.

Continued ...

Calculator Menus and Options:

Menu	Calculator menu items	Description
Edit	**Copy**	Copies displayed number to Clipboard.
	Paste	Inserts a number or equation from Clipboard to Calculator's display.
View	**Scientific**	Opens Scientific Calculator.
	Standard	Opens Standard Calculator.

Basic Calculator Functions
FOR STANDARD AND SCIENTIFIC CALCULATORS

Function	Button	Key
Add	+	+
Calculate	=	= or Enter
Calculate reciprocal	1/x	R
Change sign of number	+ —	F9
Clear displayed number or function	CE	Del
Clear calculator	C	Esc
Decimal point	.	. or ,
Delete last number entered	BACK	Bksp
Divide	/	/
Multiply	*	*
Percentage (calculate)*	%	%
Square root of displayed number*	sqrt	@
Subtract	—	—
Memory Functions		
Add displayed number to memory value .	M+	Ctrl + P
Clear memory	MC	Ctrl + L
Display contents of memory	MR	Ctrl + R
Store number in memory	MS	Ctrl + M

Applies only to Standard Calculator.

Continued ..

Scientific Calculator Functions

Scientific Functions	Button	Key
Number Systems		
Decimal	Dec	F6
Sets trigonometric input to: (when in Decimal mode)		
degrees	Deg	F2
gradients	Grad	F4
radians	Rad	F3
Binary	Bin	F8
Hexadecimal	Hex	F5
Octal	Oct	F7
Displays representation of number in: (when in Binary, Hexadecimal or Octal mode)		
Byte (lower 8 bits)	Byte	F4
Dword (full 32 bits)	Dword	F2
Word (lower 16 bits)	Word	F3
Logical Operators		
Bit shift (left one bit)	Lsh	<
Bit shift inverse (right one bit)	Inv + Lsh	i + <
Calculate bitwise inverse	Not	~
Calculate bitwise exclusive OR	Xor	^
Calculate bitwise OR	Or	|
Calculate bitwise AND	And	&
Displays remainder of division operation .	Mod	%
Integer	Int	;
Integer (fraction)	Inv + Int	i + ;
Level of calculation ( )	( )	( )

Continued...

Scientific Functions	Button	Key
Statistical Functions		
Calculate:		
mean	Ave	Ctrl + A
mean of the squares	Inv + Ave	i + Ctrl + A
standard deviation (pop. = n)	Inv + s	i + Ctrl + D
standard deviation (pop. = n - 1) . .	s	Ctrl + D
sum	Sum	Ctrl + T
sum of squares	Inv + Sum	i + Ctrl + T
Open Statistics Box:	Sta	Ctrl + S
change number in calculator display to selected number	L̲OAD	Alt + L
delete all numbers	CA̲D	Alt + A
delete currently selected number . . .	C̲D	Alt + C
enter number displayed from calculator	Dat	Insert
switch to main calculator (and retain Statistic Box entries) . .	R̲ET	Alt + R

Continued ...

Other Scientific Functions

Functions	Button	Key
Calculate:		
10 raised to x^n power	Inv + log	i + l
arc cosine	Inv + cos	i + o
arc sine	Inv + sin	i + s
arc tangent	Inv + tan	i + t
arc hyperbolic cosine	Inv + Hyp + cos	i + h + o
arc hyperbolic sine	Inv + Hyp + sin	i + h + s
arc hyperbolic tangent	Inv + Hyp + tan	i + h + t
common logarithm (base 10)	log	l
cosine	cos	o
cube	x^3	#
cube root	Inv + x^3	i + #
e raised to x^n power	Inv + ln	i + n
factorial	n!	!
hyperbolic cosine	Hyp + cos	h + o
hyperbolic sine	Hyp + sin	h + s
hyperbolic tangent	Hyp + tan	h + t
natural logarithm (base e)	ln	n
sine	sin	s
square	x^2	@
square root	Inv + x^2	i + @
tangent	tan	t
x raised to y^n power	x^y	y
y^n root of x	Inv + x^y	i + y
Degree-minute-second format	dms	m
Inverse function (set function to)	Inv	i
Pi (input value of)	PI	p
Pi times 2 (input value of)	Inv + PI	i + p
Scientific notation (set entry mode to) . . .	Exp	x
Scientific notation (toggle on and off) . . .	F - E	v

CALENDAR

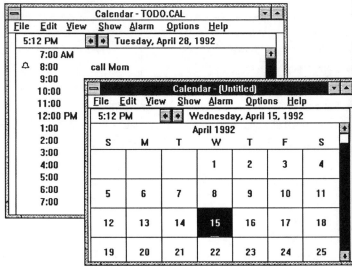

Daily and monthly views of Calendar

Start Calendar by double-clicking on the Calendar program icon in the Accessories group window. (See Running an Application from a Group Window, page 12.)

With Calendar, the user may

- Enter and edit appointments and notes.
- Set alarms for appointment times.
- Cut, copy and paste data to and from the Clipboard.
- Choose between daily and monthly calendars.
- Mark special dates on the monthly calendar.
- Print appointments.

Continued ..

Calendar Menus and Options:

Menu	Calendar menu items	Description
File	**New**	Starts a new, untitled file.
	Open...	Opens a file stored on disk.
	Save	Saves file.
	Save As...	Saves and renames current file.
	Print...	Prints and provides for selection of appointment dates to be printed.
	Page Setup...	Provides for setting of margins and inclusion of headers and footers.
	Print Setup...	Provides for selection and setup of printer.
	Exit	Exits Calendar program.
Edit	**Cut**	Removes and transfers selected text to Clipboard.
	Copy	Copies selected text to Clipboard.
	Paste	Inserts transferred text from Clipboard into appointment time slot.
	Remove...	Provides for removal of a specified range of appointment dates.
View	**Day**	Shows daily appointment times and items.
	Month	Shows all dates in current month.

Continued ...

Menu	Calendar menu items	Description
Show	**T**oday	Shows current appointment day.
	Previous	Shows previous appointment day or month.
	Next	Shows next appointment day or month.
	Date...	Changes appointment date to a specific date.
Alarm	**S**et	Sets alarm in appointment calendar at cursor position.
	Controls...	Provides for alarm settings.
Options	**M**ark...	Provides for selection of mark options for any day in monthly calendar.
	Special Time...	Provides for insertions of a special time (between preset intervals) in appointment calendar.
	Day Settings...	Provides for selection of intervals between appointments, default starting time for appointments, and hour format (12 or 24 hour clock).

CARDFILE

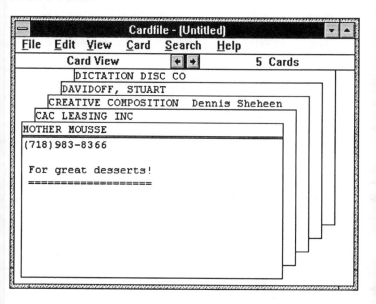

Start Cardfile by double-clicking on the Cardfile program icon in the Accessories group window. (See Running an Application from a Group Window, page 12.)

With Cardfile, the user may

- Enter and edit data on index cards.
- Cut, copy and paste text or graphics to and from the Clipboard.
- Sort cards automatically.
- Merge two Cardfile files.
- Dial phone numbers. (This requires a modem.)
- Search for cards containing specified text.
- Print a single card or entire cardfile.
- Embed or link an object into a card.

Continued ...

Cardfile Menus and Options:

Menu	Cardfile menu items	Description
File	**New**	Starts a new, untitled file.
	Open...	Opens a file stored on disk.
	Save	Saves file.
	Save As...	Saves and renames current file.
	Print	Prints front card in file.
	Print All	Prints entire file.
	Page Setup...	Provides for settings of margins and inclusion of headers and footers.
	Print Setup...	Provides for selection and setup of printer.
	Merge...	Combines a Cardfile file stored on disk with current file.
	Exit	Exits Cardfile program.
Edit	**Undo**	Restores previous deletion.
	Cut	Removes and transfers selected data to Clipboard.
	Copy	Copies selected data to Clipboard.
	Paste	Inserts data on Clipboard to card.
	Paste Link	Links data on Clipboard to card.
	Paste Special...	Provides paste format options.
	Index...	Provides for entering and editing front card's index line.
	Restore	Restores front card to condition prior to recent changes.
	Text	Sets editing mode to text.
	Picture	Sets editing mode to picture. (Enables pasting and positioning of a graphic.)
	Link...	Provides controls for links.
	Object	Provides for choosing an application used to create an object.
	Insert Object...	Provides list of applications that support object linking and embedding.

Continued..

Menu	Cardfile menu items	Description
View	**Card**	Shows cards as series of cards in the Cardfile window.
	List	Displays, in alphabetical order, index line of every card. Any index line can be selected for editing.
Card	**Add...**	Adds new card and provides for entry of index line.
	Delete	Deletes front card from file.
	Duplicate	Makes duplicate of front card.
	Autodial...	Automatically dials selected phone number on front card and provides for setup of modem.
Search	**Go To...**	Brings specified card to the front.
	Find...	Finds card containing specified text.
	Find Next	Finds next card containing previous "Find" specification.

CHARACTER MAP

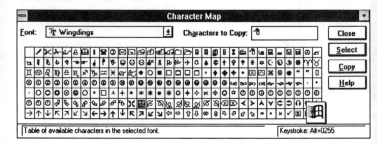

Start Character Map by double-clicking on the Character Map program icon in the Accessories group window. (See Running an Application from a Group Window, page 12.)

With Character Map, the user may insert special characters into any Windows document.

Character Map provides no menu options.

To insert a character into a document:

*   To change the font character set, click on <u>F</u>ont: ⬇, then click on desired font name.

*   To see an enlarged view of a character, point to a character and click and hold mouse button.

*   To select a character, double-click on that character. Repeat this step for each character to copy. (Selected characters appear in Characters to Copy text box.)

*   To copy character(s) to Clipboard, click on ▐ **<u>C</u>opy** ▌.

*   Select application containing document into which character(s) will be pasted.

*   Place insertion point and select same font selected in Character Map.

*   To insert the character(s), click on <u>E</u>dit, then click on <u>P</u>aste.

CLOCK

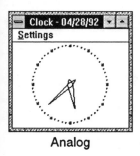

Analog

Digital

Start Clock by double-clicking on the Clock program icon in the Accessories group window. (See Running an Application from a Group Window, page 12.)

Clock Menus and Options:

Menu	Clock menu items	Description
Settings	**Analog**	Shows analog display of time.
	Digital	Shows digital display of time. (Effective when Clock is minimized.)
	Set Font...	Provides font options for digital display.
	No Title	Hides display of title and menu.
	Seconds	Includes seconds in time display.
	Date	Includes date in time display.

NOTE: To ensure that the Clock is never hidden by other windows, click on the Clock's Control-menu button, then click on Always on Top to select.

MEDIA PLAYER

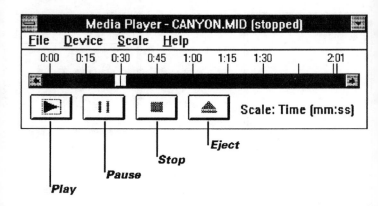

Media Player requires sound hardware and an installed and configured sound driver. Start Media Player by double-clicking on the Media Player program icon in the Accessories group window. (See Running an Application from a Group Window, page 12.)

With Media Player, the user may

- Play multimedia files, such as sound or animation files.
- Control multimedia hardware devices.

Media Player Menus and Options:

Menu	Media Player menu items	Description
File	**Open...**	Opens a file stored on disk.
	Exit	Exits Media Player program.
Device	Options vary	Provides a way to specify the MCI device to play.
Scale	**Time**	Shows time intervals.
	Tracks	Shows track locations.

NOTEPAD

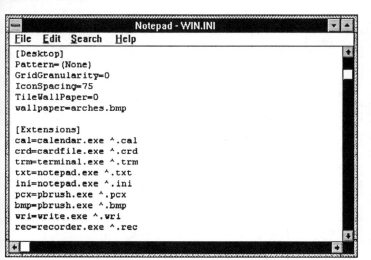

Start Notepad by double-clicking on the Notepad program icon in the Accessories group window. (See Running an Application from a Group Window, page 12.)

With Notepad, the user may

- Create and edit ASCII text files.*
- Cut, copy and paste text to and from the Clipboard.
- Search for specified text.
- Insert the system time and date into document.
- Set word wrap on or off.
- Apply page format commands, including margins, headers and footers.
- Print documents.

*NOTE: By default, files created with Notepad are in ASCII format. An ASCII text file is a standard file format. Notepad is especially useful for editing batch (.BAT) files and Windows (.INI) files.

Continued ...

Notepad Menus and Options:

Menu	Notepad menu items	Description
File	**New**	Starts a new, untitled file.
	Open...	Opens a file stored on disk.
	Save	Saves file.
	Save As...	Saves and renames current file.
	Print	Prints file.
	Page Setup...	Provides for settings of margins and inclusion of headers and footers.
	Print Setup...	Provides for selection and setup of printer.
	Exit	Exits Notepad program.
Edit	**Undo**	Restores previous deletion.
	Cut	Removes and transfers selected text to Clipboard.
	Copy	Copies selected text to Clipboard.
	Paste	Inserts transferred text from Clipboard into document.
	Delete	Deletes selected text.
	Select All	Selects all text in document.
	Time/Date	Inserts time and date at cursor position.
	Word Wrap	Turns word wrap on or off.
Search	**Find...**	Searches document for specified text.
	Find Next	Continues search using previous search criteria.

PAINTBRUSH

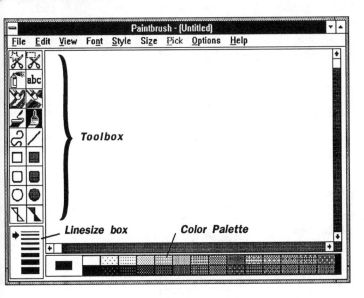

Start Paintbrush by double-clicking on the Paintbrush program icon in the Accessories group window. (See Running an Application from a Group Window, page 12.)

The Paintbrush window includes these boxes:

- Toolbox — used to select modes for creating and editing a drawing (see table on following page).
- Linesize box — used to select drawing width.
- Color Palette box — used to select color or pattern.

With Paintbrush, the user may

- Create and edit bitmap graphics and text.
- Cut, copy and paste sections of drawings to the Clipboard.
- Select a variety of fonts and font sizes.
- Magnify drawings for detailed editing.
- Print drawings.
- Link or embed objects (drawings or parts of a drawing) into other applications.

Continued ...

Paintbrush Toolbox Options

Before beginning a drawing, select a tool from the Toolbox by clicking on it, or use cursor keys to highlight desired tool, then press Insert. The Brush tool is selected when Paintbrush is started. The pointer will change depending upon the tool selected.

Scissors		Pick
Airbrush		Text
Color Eraser		Eraser
Paint Roller		Brush
Curve		Line
Box		Filled Box
Rounded Box		Filled Rounded Box
Circle/Ellipse		Filled Circle/Ellipse
Polygon		Filled Polygon

Continued ...

Paintbrush Menus and Options:

Menu	Paintbrush menu items	Description
File	**New**	Starts a new, untitled file.
	Open...	Opens a file stored on disk.
	Save	Saves file.
	Save As...	Saves, names and selects format of current file.
	Page Setup...	Provides for setting of margins and inclusion of headers and footers.
	Print...	Prints and selects print options for file.
	Print Setup...	Provides for selection and setup of printer.
	Exit	Exits Paintbrush program.
Edit	**Undo**	Removes recent changes to drawing.
	Cut	Removes and transfers to Clipboard a section of drawing selected with Cutout tool.
	Copy	Copies a section of drawing selected with Cutout tool to Clipboard.
	Paste	Inserts transferred data from Clipboard into drawing.
	Copy To...	Copies a section of drawing selected with Cutout tool.
	Paste From...	Inserts a graphic file stored on disk into current drawing.
View	**Zoom In**	Magnifies portion of drawing.
	Zoom Out	Shrinks drawing to fit in workspace.
	View Picture	Displays drawing on entire screen.
	Tools and Linesize	Shows or hides Toolbox and Linesize box.
	Palette	Shows or hides Palette.
	Cursor Position	Shows or hides cursor coordinates.

Continued ...

Menu	Paintbrush menu items	Description
Text	**R**egular	Removes all text attributes.
	Bold	Adds/removes bold text attribute.
	Italic	Adds/removes italic text attribute.
	Underline	Adds/removes underline text attribute.
	Outline	Adds/removes outline to text using selected background color.
	Shadow	Adds/removes shadow to text using selected background color.
	Fonts...	Provides for selection of a font and font size.
Pick	Flip **H**orizontal	Flips a section of drawing selected with Cutout tool from side to side.
	Flip **V**ertical	Flips a section of drawing selected with Cutout tool from top to bottom.
	Inverse	Inverts colors in a section of drawing selected with Cutout tool.
	Shrink & Grow	Shrinks or enlarges a section of drawing selected with Cutout tool.
	Tilt	Angles a section of drawing selected with Cutout tool.
	Clear	Erases original drawing and replaces with new drawing after Shrink & Grow or Tilt command.
Options	**I**mage Attributes...	Changes size of drawing area. Selects unit of measure. Selects color or black and white.
	Brush Shapes...	Changes shape of Brush tool.
	Edit Colors...	Customizes Palette colors.
	Get Colors...	Replaces current Palette with a saved Palette file.
	Save Colors...	Saves color changes in Palette to disk file.
	Omit Picture Format	Limits drawing formats transferred to Clipboard.

SOUND RECORDER

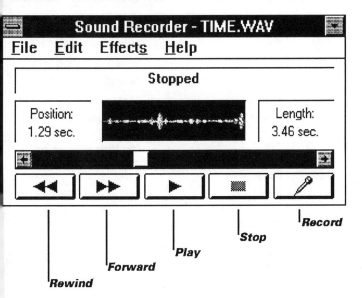

Sound Recorder requires sound hardware and an installed and
configured sound driver. Start Sound Recorder by double-clicking on
the Sound Recorder program icon in the Accessories group window.
(See Running an Application from a Group Window, page 12.)
With Sound Recorder, the user may

- Play sound files.
- Record and edit sound files.
- Modify sound files by inserting or mixing other sound files.
- Add echos and increase or decrease volume and playback
  speed.
- Reverse playback of sound files.
- Link or embed sound files (objects) into other applications.

Continued ...

Sound Recorder Menus and Options:

Menu	Sound Recorder menu items	Description
File	**New**	Starts a new, untitled file.
	Open...	Opens a file stored on disk.
	Save	Saves file.
	Save As...	Saves and renames current file.
	Revert	Returns current file to its last saved state.
	Exit	Exits Media Player program.
Edit	**Copy**	Copies sound file to Clipboard.
	Insert File...	Inserts a sound file into current sound file.
	Mix with File...	Mixes a sound file with current sound file.
	Delete Before Current Position	Deletes beginning of sound file from current position.
	Delete After Current Position	Deletes end of sound file from current position.
Effects	**Increase Volume (by 25%)**	Increases volume of sound.
	Decrease Volume	Decreases volume of sound.
	Increase Speed (by 100%)	Increases speed of playback.
	Decrease Speed	Decreases speed of playback.
	Add Echo	Adds echo effect.
	Reverse	Sets sound to play backwards.

TERMINAL

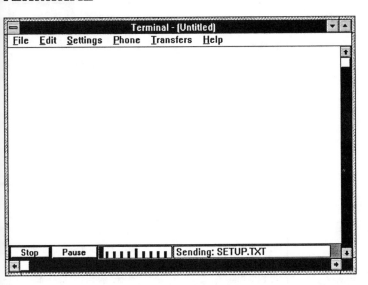

Terminal is a telecommunications package used to communicate with other computers. Terminal requires a compatible modem, an unused serial port and access to a telephone line. Start Terminal by double-clicking on the Terminal program icon in the Accessories group window. (See Running an Application from a Group Window, page 12.)

With Terminal, the user may

- Enter communication settings to match a remote computer's requirements.
- Dial remote computers.
- Execute logging-on procedures (for example, the entry of a user identification number and password when accessing an information service).
- Transfer and receive files between remote computers.
- Receive and send electronic mail.
- Execute logging-off procedures.
- Disconnect phone connection.
- Save communication settings in a Terminal (.TRM) file for future use.

Continued ...

Terminal Menus and Options:

Menu	Terminal menu items	Description
File	**New**	Starts a new settings file.
	Open...	Opens a saved settings file.
	Save	Saves a settings file.
	Save As...	Saves and renames a settings file.
	Print Setup...	Provides for selection and setup of printer.
	Exit	Exits Terminal program.
Edit	**Copy**	Copies selected text to Clipboard.
	Paste	Sends copy of Clipboard contents to remote computer.
	Send	Sends selected text to remote computer.
	Select All	Selects entire text in Terminal buffer.
	Clear Buffer	Clears contents of Terminal buffer.
Settings	**Phone Number...**	Provides for entry of phone number and dials connection settings.
	Terminal Emulations...	Provides emulation options required by remote computer.
	Terminal Preferences...	Controls screen characteristics.
	Function Keys...	Assigns keys to frequently used commands and phrases.
	Text Transfers...	Sets text transfer parameters.
	Binary Transfers...	Selects binary transfer protocol.
	Communications...	Sets communication parameters.
	Modem Commands...	Sets modem defaults and commands.
	Printer Echo	Sets option to send communications to printer.
	Timer Mode	Sets on-line timer on or off.
	Show Function Keys	Shows or hides display of function keys and system time.

Continued ..

Menu	Terminal menu items	Description
Phone	**Dial**	Dials number specified in Phone Number option.
	Hangup	Hangs up modem.
Transfers	**Send Text File...**	Provides for selection of text file and sends selected text file.
	Receive Text File...	Provides for naming and reception of text file.
	View Text File...	Displays contents of files to be sent or files received.
	Send Binary File...	Provides for selection of binary file and sends selected file in binary format.
	Receive Binary File...	Provides for naming and reception of a binary file.
	Pause	Interrupts transfer of a file.
	Resume	Continues transfer of a file that has been interrupted.
	Stop	Aborts transfer of a file.

WRITE

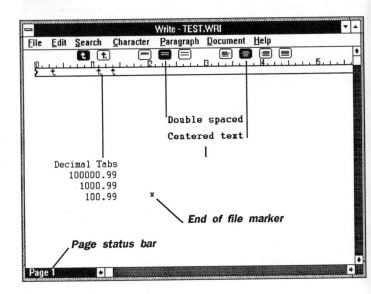

Write is a word processing application used to create, format and print documents. Start Write by double-clicking on the Write program icon in the Accessories group window. (See Running an Application from a Group, page 12.)

With Write, the user may

- Enter and edit text.
- Cut, copy and paste data to and from the Clipboard.
- Search for and replace text.
- Export text files in different formats.
- Import, size and move graphics.
- Apply page format commands, including font selection and emphasis, paragraph alignment, spacing, margins, tabs, indents, headers and footers.
- Use automatic page breaks.
- Print documents.

Continued

Write Menus and Options:

Menu	Write menu items	Description
File	**New**	Starts a new, untitled file.
	Open...	Opens a file stored on disk.
	Save	Saves file.
	Save As...	Saves, names and selects format and backup option for current file.
	Print...	Prints and selects print options for file.
	Print Setup...	Provides for selection and setup of printer.
	Repaginate...	Creates page breaks and provides repagination options.
	Exit	Exits Write program.
Edit	**Undo**	Restores previous deletion.
	Cut	Removes and transfers selected data to Clipboard.
	Copy	Copies selected data to Clipboard.
	Paste	Inserts data on Clipboard to document.
	Paste Special...	Provides paste format options.
	Paste Link	Links data on Clipboard to document.
	Links...	Provides controls for links.
	Object	Provides for choosing an application used to create an object.
	Insert Object...	Provides list of applications that support object linking and embedding.
	Move Picture	Moves a selected graphic horizontally in document.
	Size Picture	Shrinks or enlarges a selected graphic.

Continued...

Menu	Write menu items	Description
Find	**Find...**	Searches document for specified text.
	Repeat Last Find	Continues search using previous search criteria.
	Replace...	Searches for specified text and replaces with new text.
	Go To Page...	Moves insertion point to a specified page number.
Character	**Regular**	Removes emphasis from selected text.
	Bold	Emphasize selected text.
	Italic	
	Underline	
	Superscript	
	Subscript	
	Reduce Font	Changes selected or new text to next smallest size.
	Enlarge Font	Changes selected or new text to next largest size.
	Fonts...	Changes selected or new text to specified font and size.
Paragraph	**Normal**	Removes paragraph alignments, spacing and indentation settings from selected text.
	Left	Provide selection of one of four paragraph alignments to new or selected text.
	Centered	
	Right	
	Justified	
	Single Space	Provide selection of one of three spacing options.
	1 1/2 Space	
	Double Space	
	Indents...	Changes indents and margins.

Continued...

Menu	Write menu items	Description
Document	**Header...**	Adds header to document.
	Footer...	Adds footer to document.
	Ruler On	Shows or hides ruler display.
	Tabs...	Adds or removes tab stops.
	Page Layout...	Changes margins, numbering and measurements for page.

KEYSTROKE EXAMPLES

Combination keys . . . . `Alt` + `X`

*Press and hold down first key (**Alt**) while pressing second key (**X**), then release both keys.*

Keys in sequence . . . . `Alt`, `X`

*Press and release first key (**Alt**), then press and release second key (**X**).*

Arrow keys . . . . `↕↔`

*Press any combination of **arrow keys** repeatedly until desired result is obtained.*

Entering a command . . . . COMMAND `↵`

Type underlined command name, then press Enter.

INSERTION POINT MOVEMENT

To move insertion point:

up one line . . . . `↑`

down one line . . . . `↓`

left one character . . . . `←`

right one character . . . . `→`

right one word . . . . `Ctrl` + `→`

left one word . . . . `Ctrl` + `←`

to beginning of line . . . . `Home`

to end of line . . . . `End`

to previous screen . . . . `PgUp`

to next screen . . . . `PgDn`

to beginning of document . . . . `Ctrl` + `Home`

to end of document . . . . `Ctrl` + `End`

TEXT SELECTION

The following keys select or extend the selection of text. Not all applications will support all of these commands.

To select or extend a selection:

one character left . . . . `Shift` + `←`

one character right . . . . `Shift` + `→`

to next line . . . . `Shift` + `↓`

to previous line . . . . `Shift` + `↑`

to end of line . . . . `Shift` + `End`

to beginning of line . . . . `Shift` + `Home`

down one screen . . . . `Shift` + `PgDn`

up one screen . . . . `Shift` + `PgUp`

to next word . . . . `Ctrl` + `Shift` + `→`

to previous word . . . . `Ctrl` + `Shift` + `←`

end of document . . . . `Ctrl` + `Shift` + `End`

beginning of document . . . . `Ctrl` + `Shift` + `Home`

EDITING – Delete, Move, Copy, Paste

Delete character to right of insertion point . . . . `Del`

Delete character to left of insertion point . . . . `BkSp`

Delete selected text . . . . `Del`

Delete selected text and transfer it
    to Clipboard . . . . `Shift` + `Del`

Copy selected text and transfer it
    to Clipboard . . . . `Ctrl` + `Ins`

Paste text from Clipboard to current insertion
    point location . . . . `Shift` + `Ins`

Continued ...

EDITING — Delete, Move, Copy, Paste (continued)

Clear contents of Clipboard . . . . `Del`

Copy entire screen to Clipboard . . . . `Prnt Scrn`
Non-Windows applications must be running in text mode.

Copy entire active window to Clipboard . . . . `Alt` + `Prnt Scrn`

Undo previous editing change . . . . `Alt` + `BkSp`

DIALOG BOX

Check Boxes

Move to a check box . . . . `Tab`

Select or deselect current check box . . . . `Space`

Command Buttons

Execute a specific command . . . . `Alt` + `X` , `↵`
where (X) represents underlined letter in command name.

Execute an outlined command . . . . `↵`

List Boxes

Open a drop-down list box . . . . `Alt` + `↓`

Move highlight up or down . . . . `↑↓`

Move highlight to first item . . . . `Home`

Move highlight to last item . . . . `End`

Extend selection up or down . . . . `Shift` + `↑↓`

Select or cancel highlighted item(s) . . . . `Space`

Select all items . . . . `Ctrl` + `/`

Scroll up or down one screen . . . . `PgUp` or `PgDn`

Cancel all extended selections . . . . `Ctrl` + `\`

Continued ...

DIALOG BOX — (continued)

Navigating

Move to next option . . . . `Tab`

Move among options within a group . . . . `⬆⬇`

Move to a specific item . . . . `Alt` + `X`
    where (X) represents underlined letter in item name.

Option Buttons

Move to an option button group . . . . `Tab`

Select an option button within a group . . . . `⬆⬇`

Text Boxes

Move insertion point left or right . . . . `⬅➡`

Move to first character . . . . `Home`

Move to last character . . . . `End`

Extend text selection one character at a time . . . . . . `Shift` + `⬆⬇`

Extend text selection to the first character . . . . `Shift` + `Home`

Extend text selection to the last character . . . . `Shift` + `End`

Other Options

Accept settings and exit dialog box . . . . `↵`
    *when **OK** command button is outlined.*

Cancel settings and exit dialog box . . . . `Esc`

MENU BAR

Activate menu bar . . . . `Alt`

Cancel menu or menu item . . . . `Esc`

Choose a specific menu item from an open pull-down menu . . `X`
    where (X) represents the underlined letter in menu item name.

Choose highlighted menu item . . . . `↵`

Move among menus on active menu bar . . . . `⇄`

Move among menu items . . . . `↕`

Open a highlighted menu . . . . `↵`

Open a specific menu on menu bar . . . . `Alt` + `X`
    where (X) represents the underlined letter in menu name.

WINDOWS APPLICATIONS

Close a selected application running in a window or
    as an icon . . . . `Alt` + `F4`

Open Task List to show all running applications . . . . . . `Ctrl` + `Esc`
    From the Task List you can switch to or close
    a specific application.

Select next application running in a window
    or as an icon . . . . `Alt` + `Esc`
    The application is not opened if it is running as an icon.

Switch to and open any running application . . . . `Alt` + `Tab`
    *Press and hold **Alt** while pressing and releasing*
    ***Tab** until desired application's name appears.*

Switch to last used application . . . . `Alt` + `Tab`

NON-WINDOWS APPLICATIONS

Return to Windows after running MS-DOS program . . . .   <u>EXIT</u> , [↵]

Return to Windows after running MS-DOS program
    and leave MS-DOS running . . . .   [Alt] + [Tab]

Switch to last used application . . . .   [Alt] + [Tab]

Switch to and open any running applications . . . .   [Alt] + [Tab]
    *Press and hold **Alt** while pressing and releasing*
    ***Tab** until desired application's name appears.*

Switch between running a non-Windows application
    in a window and running it full-screen . . . .   [Alt] + [↵]

CONTROLLING APPLICATION WINDOWS AND ICONS

Arrange application windows in
    side-by-side order (Tile) . . . .   [Ctrl] + [Esc] , [Alt] + [T]

Arrange application windows in
    overlapping order (Cascade) . . . .   [Ctrl] + [Esc] , [Alt] + [C]

Arrange application icons . . . .   [Ctrl] + [Esc] , [Alt] + [A]

Close a selected application's Control-menu . . . .   [Alt]

Minimize a selected application window . . . . . .   [Alt] + [Space] , [N]

Maximize a selected application window . . . . . .   [Alt] + [Space] , [X]

Move a selected application
    window or icon . . . .   [Alt] + [Space] , [M] , [↕↔] , [↵]
    Press arrow keys until item is in desired location.

Continued ...

CONTROLLING APPLICATION WINDOWS AND ICONS (continued)

Open a selected application's Control-menu .... `Alt` + `Space`

Open and restore a selected application icon
    to its previous size .... `Alt` + `Space` , `R`

Open and maximize a selected application icon
    to its largest size .... `Alt` + `Space` , `X`

Restore a selected maximized application window
    to its previous size .... `Alt` + `Space` , `R`

Size a selected application
    window .... `Alt` + `Space` , `S` , `↕` , `↕` , `↵`
Press any arrow key <u>once</u> in direction of border to size, then press arrow keys until desired size is obtained. Repeat all keystrokes for each border to size.

CONTROLLING DOCUMENT WINDOWS AND ICONS

Document windows are windows that belong to and are contained within an application (i.e., group windows in Program Manager and directory windows in File Manager).

Arrange document icons .... `Alt` + `W` , `A`

Arrange document windows in overlapping
    order (Cascade) .... `Shift` + `F5`

Arrange document windows in side-by-side
    order (Tile) .... `Shift` + `F4`

Close a selected document window or icon .... `Ctrl` + `F4`

Close Control-menu of selected document window or icon .... `Alt`

Open Control-menu of selected document window or icon. `Alt` + `-`

Continued ...

CONTROLLING DOCUMENT WINDOWS AND ICONS
(continued)

Open a selected document icon and
    restore it to its previous size . . . . `Alt`+`—`, `R`

Open and maximize a selected document icon
    to its largest size . . . . `Alt`+`—`, `X`

Maximize a selected document window . . . . `Alt`+`—`, `X`

Minimize a selected document window . . . . `Alt`+`—`, `N`

Move a selected document
    window or icon . . . . `Alt`+`—`, `M`, `↕`, `↵`
    Press arrow keys until item is in desired location.

Move among items in a document window . . . . `↕`

Restore a maximized document window
    to its previous size . . . . `Alt`+`—`, `R`

Size a selected document window . `Alt`+`—`, `S`, `↕`, `↕`, `↵`
    Press any arrow key <u>once</u> in direction of border to size, then
    press arrow keys until desired size is obtained. Repeat all
    keystrokes for each border to size.

Select next document window
    or document icon . . . . `Ctrl`+`Tab` or `Ctrl`+`F6`
    *Press and hold **Ctrl** while pressing and releasing **Tab** or **F6***
    until desired document title is highlighted.

Switch to a specific document . . . . `Alt`+`W`, `¼`, `↵`
    Press up or down key until a document name is highlighted.

FILE MANAGER

Directory Window
Also see Controlling Document Windows and Icons, above.

Move between directory areas . . . . `Tab`

Continued ...

FILE MANAGER (continued)

Drive Area

Change current drive in active directory window . . . . . . `Ctrl` + `X`
where (X) represents the letter of desired drive.

Open a new window for a drive . . . . `Tab` , `↹` , `↵`

Directory Tree Area

Collapse current directory . . . . `—`

Copy selected directory . . . . `F8`

Delete selected directory . . . . `Del`

Expand current directory . . . . `+`

Move selected directory . . . . `F7`

Open a directory . . . . `↵`

Open a window displaying the contents of
    selected directory . . . . `Shift` + `↵`

Refresh directory tree list . . . . `F5`

Select directory listed above or below current directory . . . . . . `↕`

Select directory listed above current subdirectory . . . . `←`

Select first directory one screen up from current directory . . . `PgUp`

Select first subdirectory listed below the current directory . . . . `→`

Select last directory in list . . . . `End`

Select last directory one screen down from current directory . `PgDn`

Select previous directory at same level . . . . `Ctrl` + `↑`

Select next directory at same level . . . . `Ctrl` + `↓`

Select the next directory whose name begins with
    specified letter or number . . . . any character

Select root directory . . . . `Home`

   or . . . . `\`

Show or hide any subdirectories . . . . `↵`

Continued ...

FILE MANAGER (continued)

Directory Contents List Area

Cancel all selections in list except current selection . . . `Ctrl` + `\`

Copy selected files and directories . . . . `F8`

Delete selected files and directories . . . . `Del`

Move selected files or directories . . . . `F7`

Open selected directory or file . . . . `⏎`

Refresh directory contents list . . . . `F5`

Run a selected application . . . . `⏎`

Select an item above or below current item . . . . `↑↓`

Select all items in list . . . . `Ctrl` + `/`

Select first item in list . . . . `Home`

Select first item one screen up from current selection . . . . . . `PgUp`

Select last item one screen down from current selection . . . . `PgDn`

Select last item in list . . . . `End`

Select next item whose name begins with

specified letter or number . . . . any character

Select or cancel a multiple selection . . . . `Shift` + `↑↓`

Select nonconsecutive items or cancel
the selections . . . . `Shift` + `F8`, `↑↓`, `Space`

Select or cancel selection of nonconsecutive items marked
by a blinking insertion point . . . . `Space`

WINDOWS — An Overview

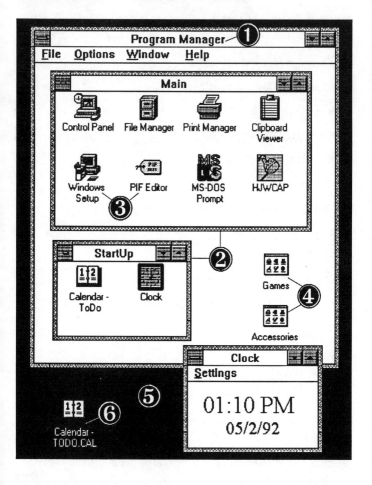

The illustration above and the text that follows describe many of the key elements and features of the Windows environment.

Continued ...

WINDOWS — An Overview (continued)

- When Windows is started, it automatically runs
  PROGRAM MANAGER[1], which runs as long as
  Windows is in use. Central to the operations in
  Windows, Program Manager helps you to organize
  and run applications.

- Program Manager's **GROUP WINDOWS**[2] contain
  PROGRAM ITEM ICONS[3] that represent installed
  applications. From a group window, you can run an
  application by double-clicking on a program item
  icon. Program item icons that are placed in a
  special group called StartUp (i.e., Clock and
  Calendar) will run automatically when you start
  Windows.

- Group windows can be reduced to **GROUP ICONS**[4]
  that can be restored when needed.

- The Program Manager window and the Clock
  window are examples of applications running in
  separate windows. As you can see, Windows lets
  you view and use more than one program at a time.
  This is called multitasking.

- Applications running in windows can be moved and
  sized and can be placed anywhere on the
  DESKTOP[5] — the area below all windows.

- A running application can be reduced to an icon.
  When minimized, it will appear on the bottom of the
  desktop as an **APPLICATION ICON**[6].

PARTS OF A WINDOW

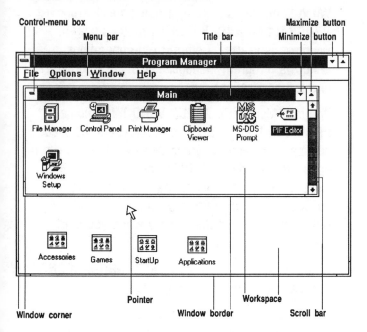

Control-menu box provides access to the Control-menu.

Maximize button opens a window to its largest size.

Minimize button reduces a window to an icon.

Menu bar provides access to application commands.

Pointer corresponds to mouse movements.

Scroll bar provides access to hidden areas of the workspace.

Title bar displays the name of a window.

Window border and **window corner** can be used to resize a window.

Workspace displays data.

SHARING DATA BETWEEN APPLICATIONS

About Clipboard

When you **cut** or **copy** selected data from within an application, the data is sent to the **Clipboard**. The **Clipboard** is a special program that provides temporary storage for this data. Data held in the Clipboard can be inserted into any application by using an application's **Paste** command.

About Object Linking and Embedding (OLE)

An **object** is any piece of data created in a Windows application, such as a drawing in Paintbrush, text in a Write document, or sound in Sound Recorder. An object can be embedded in or linked to another application.

Object Embedding is a way to copy an object from a source application (e.g., Paintbrush) into a receiving application document (e.g., Write) so it can be edited directly from the program that received the object.

Object Linking connects an object that has been copied from a source application and embedded in one or more receiving documents. You can edit a linked object directly from any document that has received the object. When a linked object is edited, you are changing the source object, and all other objects that are linked to the same object are updated automatically.

About Object Packaging

Object Packaging is another way to embed or link an object. This process embeds an icon — a package that represents the object — instead of the actual object. When you choose the package, the application used to create the object opens and displays or plays back the object.

PARTS OF A DIALOG BOX

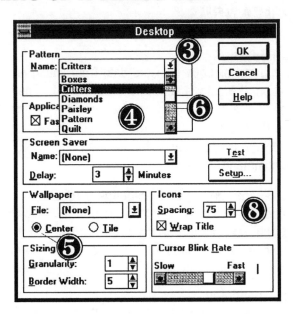

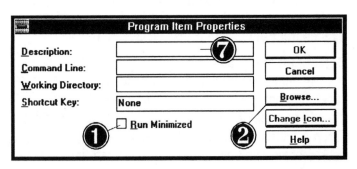

- A **CHECK BOX**[1] provides for selection or deselection of options. A selected check box contains an **X**. More than one check box may be selected at a time.

- A **COMMAND BUTTON**[2] executes a command.

- A **DROP-DOWN LIST ARROW**[3] opens a drop-down list from which selections can be made.

Continued ...

PARTS OF A DIALOG BOX (continued)

- A **LIST BOX**[4] displays a list of items from which selections can be made.

- An **OPTION BUTTON**[5] provides for selection of an option. A selected option button contains a dark circle. Only one option in a group may be selected.

- A **SCROLL BAR**[6] provides access to hidden items in a list box.

- A **TEXT BOX**[7] provides a space to type information required to carry out a command.

- **INCREMENT ARROWS**[8] provide for increasing or decreasing a value in an increment box.

FILE MANAGER — An Overview

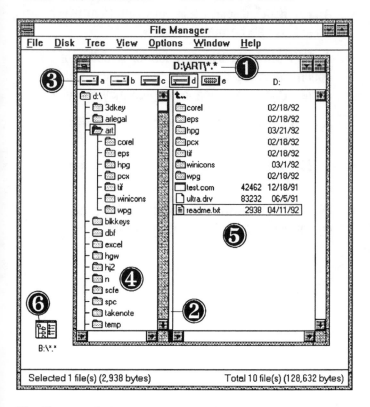

File Manager helps you manage files stored in directories on your system's disk drives. When you first start File Manager, the File Manager window and a directory window appear.

PARTS OF THE DIRECTORY WINDOW

- The directory window's **TITLE BAR**[1] shows the path to the current directory. "D:" represents the current drive, "\ART" indicates the current directory, and "*.*" indicates that all files are shown.

- A movable **SPLIT BAR**[2] separates the directory tree and the directory contents list.

FILE MANAGER — An Overview (continued)

The Drive Area

- The **DRIVE AREA**[3] displays your system's disk drives as **drive icons** (i.e., 🖴). A rectangle surrounds the **current disk drive**.

The Directory Tree

- The **DIRECTORY TREE**[4] shows the directory structure for the current drive. The 📁 **d:** (root directory) at the top of the directory tree indicates the first level of the directory structure from which all subdirectories branch. The 📂 (open directory folder) indicates the **current directory**.

The Directory Contents List

- The **DIRECTORY CONTENTS LIST**[5] shows the files and any subdirectories contained in the current directory. The ⬆🗀 (up icon) indicates the way to the **parent directory** of the current directory listing.

- ▭ (an application icon) indicates that the file is a **program file** that can be executed.

- 📄 (an associated data file icon) indicates that the filename extension for that file has been **associated** with a particular application file.

- 📄 (a document icon) indicates that the file is not an application and that it has not been associated with an application.

Directory Icon

- More than one directory window can be opened at a time. A directory window can be reduced to a **DIRECTORY ICON**[6].

Continued ...

Continued ...

Continued ...

Continued ...

Continued ...

Continued ...

Continued ...

INDEX

More Quick Reference Guides

Did we make one for you?